CAD of
Concurrent Computers

ELECTRONIC & ELECTRICAL ENGINEERING RESEARCH STUDIES

COMPUTER ENGINEERING SERIES

Series Editor: **Professor F. G. Heath,** *Heriot-Watt University, Scotland*

CAD of Concurrent Computers

Patrick W. Foulk
Senior Lecturer in Computer Engineering
Heriot-Watt University, Scotland
and
Chief Design Consultant
Memex Information Engines Ltd.

RESEARCH STUDIES PRESS LTD.
Letchworth, Hertfordshire, England
JOHN WILEY & SONS INC.
New York · Chichester · Toronto · Brisbane · Singapore

RESEARCH STUDIES PRESS LTD.
58B Station Road, Letchworth, Herts. SG6 3BE, England

Marketing and Distribution:

Australia, New Zealand, South-east Asia:
Jacaranda-Wiley Ltd., Jacaranda Press
JOHN WILEY & SONS INC.
GPO Box 859, Brisbane, Queensland 4001, Australia

Canada:
JOHN WILEY & SONS CANADA LIMITED
22 Worcester Road, Rexdale, Ontario, Canada

Europe, Africa:
JOHN WILEY & SONS LIMITED
Baffins Lane, Chichester, West Sussex, England

North and South America and the rest of the world:
JOHN WILEY & SONS INC.
605 Third Avenue, New York, NY 10158, USA

Library of Congress Cataloging in Publication Data

Foulk, Patrick W., 1945–
    CAD of concurrent computers.

    (Electronic & electrical engineering research studies.
Computer engineering series; 4)
    Bibliography: p.
    Includes index.
    1. System design.   2. Computer-aided design.
3. Electronic digital computers—Design and construction.
4. Parallel processing (Electronic computers)   I. Title.
II. Series: Electronic & electrical engineering research
studies. Computer engineering series; no. 4.
QA76.9.S88F68 1985   620'.00425'02854   85-8217
ISBN 0 471 90792 8 (Wiley)

British Library Cataloguing in Publication Data

Foulk, Patrick W.
    CAD of concurrent computers.—(Electronic &
    electrical engineering research studies. Computer
    engineering series; 4)
    1. Computer architecture—Data processing
    I. Title   II. Series
    001.64   QA76.9.A73

    ISBN 0 86380 030 0

    ISBN 0 86380 030 0 (Research Studies Press Ltd.)
    ISBN 0 471 90792 8 (John Wiley & Sons Inc.)

Printed in Great Britain by Short Run Press Ltd., Exeter

To Hilary

Acknowledgements

I would like to thank all those people who have been involved in the IDES project over the years. In particular, Patrick O'Callaghan for his work on the G language, Alan Mason for his work on HDL, and especially John McLean for his work on the integrated circuit database and his encouragement and help in producing this book. Professor Heath has generously contributed his time, knowledge, and experience to the many discussions we have had on concurrency. Some of the work has been funded by the Science and Engineering Research Council, while The Royal Society and The Carnegie Trust have also contributed to travel and study costs.

P.W.F.

Series Editor's Foreword

During the period 1960-70 there was a great explosion in the design of digital machinery and software. The ambitions and plans of computer companies ran far ahead of any theoretical or methodical design methods, leading to one or two spectacular failures as well as general frustration between users and makers. Structured programming and design automation (CAD for computer hardware) were two ideas which sprang directly from these difficulties, but only managed to alleviate them.

It was towards the end of this period, and after many talks with Dr. E.L. Glaser, then of MIT, that two things became obvious to me. The first was that something had to be done about applying computers to the design process (not just the drawing-office and programming environment), and also that of all the professional people, computer designers and programmers were resisting the use of computers in their heartland most vigorously.

As formal methods have developed, their use has certainly not been welcomed. It is only the increasing need for parallelism in the programming and system areas which has brought about an appreciation of the various possibilities. For instance, if Christopher Strachey's theorem, that no computation can be proved correct by examining its structure alone, is taken literally, one may think that exhaustive simulation (and in this field exhaustive is often exactly that) is the only way to prove a CPU or program. In fact, by using the techniques in this book, exhaustive simulation can be cut down to size by the proof of correctness in modules which can then be nested down to any chosen level.

After examining the current state of activity, it seemed to Dr. Foulk and myself that the time had come to distil all the work done in Case Western Reserve and Heriot-Watt Universities into one readable text which attempts to show the possibilities for checking logical correctness in computational structures and indicates the possibilities for concurrent operation. The text gives many personal and institutional references, so I will not repeat them here: sufficient to say that working systems have been demonstrated in CWRU and HWU which create a good mental environment for the design of hardware and software.

One part of the book, Chapter 6, is particularly the work of Dr. Foulk and his team. It covers the successful transformation of TTL electronic specifications so that a database can be created which relates TTL components to the natural processes within the directed-graph system. I believe this technique, with modifications to suit the case, has wide application.

Finally, perhaps I should say something for designers who cannot get a directed graph CAD system for their work. An appreciation of the methods in this book will improve your normal design or programming skill whenever concurrency is met. Even the simple fact that parallel processors cannot do anything with a single-stream algorithm doesn't seem to be appreciated in some circles!

F.G.Heath.

Table of Contents

Table of Figures

CHAPTER 1

Computer-Aided Design

1.1   THE DESIGN AUTOMATION PROCESS

The design of digital systems is an extremely complex and involved task. For any given target specification, there are usually a large number of ways of meeting it, each having both good and bad features. Frequently there is dispute as to what the specification actually means, and whether the final design meets that specification. This is the result of several factors. Firstly, there is no universally accepted specification language for digital systems which is at a sufficiently high level to permit the meaningful and understandable description of a complex system without having designed the system first. Secondly, the design process is usually a blend of intuition, insight, inspiration, guesswork and experience. It is not a closely defined process whereby a specification is turned into hardware using a defined translation algorithm. Thirdly, the verification process whereby it should be shown that the design meets the specification is extremely difficult to apply across the variety of different ways in which the design is represented during the translation from specification to actual hardware. Fourthly, the specification frequently changes as the design proceeds, since the design process itself often reveals inadequacies in the specification.

It is these factors which make the design of digital systems so challenging, and the design of a digital systems computer-aided design system so difficult. Clearly, one of the goals for such a design system must be that of being an integrated system covering all levels and aspects of the design process, relating them to each other in a determinate way.

Such a system should be used to specify the target digital system. It should be used by the designer to interactively design the digital system, enabling him to rapidly investigate different implementation approaches, hardware vs software advantages etc. It should be hierarchical in that sections of the design should be capable of being designed and then incorporated into the design, or it should be possible to leave the detailed design of some sections until later. Several designers should be able to work on and communicate about a common design task. To this end the design system should impose a benign framework of design constraints and formations on users. It should ease the task of producing correctly functioning designs, ease the tasking of those designs, and ease the unpopular job of correctly documenting the design. It would also be advantageous if the descriptions of hardware provided a medium for communicating designs between various hardware and software engineers, and as a tool for teaching digital design.

Most digital systems and integrated circuit manufacturers have adequately automated procedures for assignment, placement, and routing, even if some manual intervention is permitted/necessary for optimised performance. They also have adequate facilities for gate level simulation and the generation of tests for simple faults. However the most difficult part of the process still to be automated is the conversion of the design specification into the programs and logic diagrams which form an input to the previously mentioned procedures.

At this point it is appropriate to differentiate between design systems and documentation systems. Many CAD systems are actually not DESIGN systems as such, but serve to document the design as the designer proceeds from initial specification to actual implementation, and the 'aid' provided by the computer may only be the performance of mechanistic algorithms. For example, a digital circuit which has been designed in terms of registers, gates etc. may be input to the computer in terms of a list of elements, identifiers, and connections. The computer-aided production of logic diagrams, wiring lists, and to some extent partioning and p.c.b. design is an extremely useful and time-saving help for the designer but does not contribute very much to the actual design process. Clearly, having this information and these procedures computerised helps the documentation of certain aspects of the design and rapidly enables modifications to be incorporated into the design. Such a CAD system has not helped the designer to do his digital system design and get it 'right'. The form in which the designer stores his design in the computer should be amenable to being used as input to a simulator so that he can check, to some extent, that the design is likely to work when mechanistically implemented via the rest of the CAD system.

A true design system should help the designer in the task of design. Thus it should identify problems in the design before the designer has proceeded too far along the design process. It should only allow 'good' designs to be expressed, or require the designer to make a conscious decision to violate the design rules. A major item in the true CAD system is a database of components for the designer to use in his implementation. This database must contain information about the components and how they are used when incorporated into a design. Software should help the designer to select components from this database and incorporate them into the design implementation by ensuring the provision of the correct signals for their operation. Thus a true design system integrates a hierarchical set of design descriptions, a database of components, and software to aid in the development, verification and correct implementation of the design.

One of the main avenues of development has been that of Computer Hardware Description Languages (CHDLs). These, as their name implies, are for the description of computer and digital hardware, and thus

more suited to the documentation role in hardware design, although
with suitable software it is possible to use them in the design role.
One of the problems with CHDLs is in their number and variety. Many
have been developed, for use at varying levels in the design process.
It is here that the problem arises, two languages at different levels
in a design are different, may even interpret the same symbols dif-
ferently (e.g. at one level + may mean ADD, at another it may mean
OR). A problem also arises in ensuring a correct translation from one
level to another, more detailed, level. Thus designers tend to use
only one language, and put up with its imperfections or develop extensions to it.

Another vital aspect of digital design is that of simulation. It is
necessary to simulate the design at various levels to ensure that it
still conforms to the original specification. Thus simulation still
needs to operate at various levels in the design process, from functional simulation at the highest level down to the gate level, and
even the silicon level at the lowest end when integrated circuits are
being made. As well as checking on the correct operation of the
design, simulation is useful for finding out what happens under various fault conditions, and is also used in the automatic test generation process to establish the correct response for various input sequences.

Testing of digital circuits is an essential task and this is also
the subject of computer aids. Whilst it is true to say that a digital
circuit must be designed with testing in mind, the generation of test
sequences and their appropriate responses is still a tedious and
time-consuming process which is amenable to aid by the computer. As
stated above, it uses simulation and so may be considered an integral
part of the simulation process.

1.2   HARDWARE DESCRIPTION LANGUAGES AND SIMULATORS

An attempt has been made to define a Consensus Language, one incorporating as many of the features of existing languages as possible. Conlan has been developed in the United States as the industry standard Consensus Language for hardware description, and as such it is simply a definition and not an implementation. So far, little of this effort seems to have percolated through to actual design systems.

CASL is a Computer Architecture Specification Language designed for hardware description at the register-transfer level. It is a state machine description language for experimenting with new computer architectures. The machine may be decomposed into cooperating asynchronous modules. The researchers at the University of Utah intend this system to produce descriptions to be compiled into microcoded simulators or to be compiled into VLSI circuits [1].

ISPS (Instruction Set Processor Simulator) is a language and simulator which is based on the ISP description language of Bell and Newell, one of the earliest hardware description languages [2]. It is a part of the Carnegie-Mellon Symbolic Manipulation of Computer Descriptions (SMCD) project. Intended for the specification, evaluation and verification of computer instruction sets, an instruction is described by a condition and an action sequence. It is for the description of behaviour rather than structure, and hence such facilities as timing are primitive. The ISPS simulator is based on an imaginary computer, the Register Transfer Machine (RTM). The simulator is a software implementation of the RTM, and executes RTM code generated by the ISPS compiler from the computer description.

The MIMOLA Design System is a synthesis tool which starts with a high level behavioural system description [3]. It generates a structural description of the digital system at the register transfer level. The Automated Logic Design System is intended to take the register transfer description and expand this to the gate level. Honeywell intend this system to be used for designing VLSI circuits.

CAP/DSDL is a Concurrent Algorithmic Programming Language/Digital

System Design Language which is based on PL/1 with numerous additional features to handle timing, interrupt handling and structural descriptions [4]. Extremely detailed delay timing is possible, and both synchronous and asynchronous systems are handled, even though the control structure is based on the timed interpreted Petri net. The CAPSIM simulator executes CAP/DSDL programs, the system having been developed at the University of Dortmund.

The Parallel Hardware Processing Language PHPL has been developed at the University of Munich [5]. This language is for the description and simulation of hardware at the architectural, register-transfer, and gate levels. The description of the hardware configuration may be hierarchically subdivided into modules and submodules. The timing may be asynchronous or synchronous and the detailed timing specifications can model gates and flip-flops accurately. The designer may state conditions to be used to check the correct logical behaviour and timing.

The Electronic Logic Language ELLA has been developed by RSRE and is marketed by SWURCC as a language for the digital hardware designer and it covers a wide range of hardware design [6]. It has facilities for describing networks, and the behaviour of nodes. Nodes may be anything from transistors to microprocessors. Ella is a non-procedural language with explicit timing, and it encourages a top-down design. The system includes a simulator.

A Design Language for Indicating Behaviour, ADLIB is a language based on PASCAL, with some ideas from SIMULA [7]. It has facilities for defining timing and behaviour of computer components, and specifying the interfaces between them. It handles synchronous and asynchronous timing. It can be used for describing software as well as hardware, and it is hierarchical over a wide range of abstractions. It is normally used with the functional simulator SABLE (Structure And Behaviour Linking Environment). This simulator combines algorithmic descriptions of the component behaviour along with structural information about its nesting and interconnections using the Structural Description Language SDL. Levels from the architectural level down through the register-transfer level to the gate and circuit level can be catered for in this system from Stanford University.

The Functional and Timing Specification Language FTL is a conventional HDL with additional statements to allow for the modelling of input/output timing specifications [8]. It was designed for modelling complex modules like microprocessors in addition to simpler components. The language is part of a gate and functional level simulation program intended to assist in design verification, FANSIM3. This is an event and table driven simulator with four logic states. It can be used for fault simulation and worst case timing analysis. It is from GTE Laboratories.

LDL, a Logic Description Language, is capable of accurately modelling the behaviour of components in a modular fashion [9]. Only one compiled model of each component exists for economy of simulator store, and the system is hierarchical, allowing abstraction. The compiler and simulator are written in the RCC system implementation language, all of which come from the University of Manchester.

HILO2 is an integrated suite of logic design tools from Cirrus Computers Ltd. [10]. It is intended for the simulation and automatic test pattern generation of digital systems. The description language allows both behavioural and structural descriptions, and is therefore multi-level. Asynchronous and synchronous systems are catered for with the detailed timing specifications. At the higher level, behavioural descriptions can be triggered by named events. The simulator is driven by a convenient waveform description input language, and is written in BCPL for portability.

An example of an integrated design system is offered by Silvar-Lisco. Founded in 1981, the company offers the SL-2000 integrated circuit design package [11]. This runs on a variety of hardware (VAX,

PRIME, IBM and APPOLLO). Designs are entered into the design database using hierarchical descriptions in a structured design language (SDL) or in schematic form using an interactive graphics terminal or a digitiser. After optional partitioning and hierarchy removal, the design database may be interfaced to logic simulators such as TEGAS, circuit simulators such as SPICE, or the mixed mode simulator DIANA. Silvar-Lisco offer HELIX high-level simulator and BIMOS bipolar/MOS logic level simulator. One design suite is GARDS for technology independent design of gate array circuits, with interactive placement optimisation, automatic routing plus a routing editor, design rule checking and interface to standard artwork generation systems such as CALMA, APPLICON and COMPUTERVISION. CAL-MP performs a similar function for standard-cell MOS and bipolar circuits. It is possible to extract physical properties from the layout for post-layout simulation. The software may be accessed via the CYBERNET timesharing network if it is not desired to purchase it.

Thus it can be seen that a great variety of design aids and specification systems are available to help digital designers. Each method or system has its merits and disadvantages which it is impossible to investigate here. References have been given to enable interested readers to discover more about the systems. The main purpose of this book is to introduce an alternative system which the author believes has a number of advantages. This system, the Integrated DEsign System, IDES, is described in the following chapters.

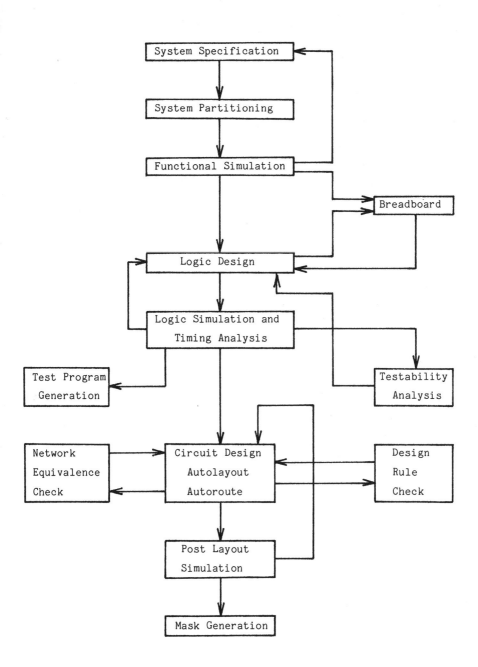

FIG 1.1.   The Electronic Design Hierarchy

CHAPTER 2

Background to the Integrated DEsign System IDES

2.1   INTRODUCTION

This book is concerned specifically with the problem of designing concurrent hardware, i.e. hardware which can potentially have several
operations active at the same time. The problem is basically that of
coordinating asynchronous parallel processes. A number of people have
addressed this problem which reduces to the correct synchronisation of
these asynchronous parallel processes. Normal flowcharts are not a
suitable representation system as they are principally concerned with
sequencing operations serially rather than co-ordinating operations in
parallel. What is needed is a representation which is suited to parallel processes, and permits analysis to ensure that these parallel
processes are interrelated and sequenced correctly. C.A. Petri [12]
developed a system for graphically portraying asynchronous events
which is is still used in some European centres. Petri nets, as they
are known, were developed to impose a communication discipline on
asynchronous operators based on local conditions, and therefore to el-
iminate the need for a global evaluation of the system state. Petri
did not attempt to develop a set of analytical tools capable of investigating the expected behaviour of Petri nets.

The paper by Karp and Miller [13] on parallel program schemata introduced a model for the representation and study of programs containing parallel sequencing. By introducing to the model information

about the memory structure, they were able to develop methods of determining the degree of parallelism in a program, and also whether it is determinate, i.e. whether the results of the computation are independent of the speeds of concurrently executed operations. Determinate systems do not exhibit the 'race-hazards' of hardware. The type of schema developed by Karp and Miller that is of interest is the counter schema, and this has been developed at MIT [14], UCLA [15], CASE [16] and Heriot-Watt [17].

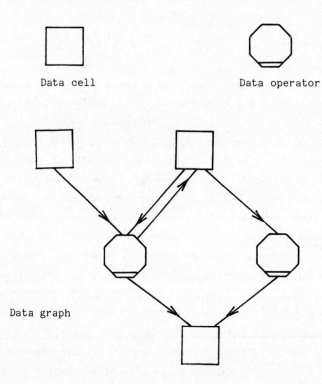

FIG. 2.1.   Data directed graph symbols

2.2   THE DIRECTED GRAPH MODEL OF COMPUTING SYSTEMS

The different models are variations on the Karp and Miller model, and
hence have some features in common. A computation is represented by
two directed graphs, a data directed graph and a control directed
graph. In its most basic form, a directed graph is simply a graph
with nodes having directed arcs between the nodes. Let us examine the
basic ideas of this model.

2.2.1   Data directed graph

The data directed graph is the mechanism whereby Karp and Miller added
the information to permit analysis of the computation, and is the main
difference from the Petri net. The nodes may be cells or operators.
The operators take information from their input cells, transform it
and supply results to their output cells (Fig. 2.1). The 'domain' of
an operator is its set of input cells. The 'range' of an operator is
its set of output cells. Cells are considered by most models to be
actual memory locations containing data, but it is possible to gen-
eralise this to consider that data cells merely represent the variable
names.

Data graphs are 'uninterpreted'. They indicate how the computations
are to be performed rather than how the algorithm is to be implemented. Thus all data operators are simply nodes with names which identify them. They simply take data from the domain cells, transform it in
some arbitrary manner, and place the results in the range cells. Thus
data operator D performs 'Operation [domain (D), range (D)]' for any
data operator. However, it is assumed that a data operator always
puts identical values into its range cells for all initiations with
identical values in its domain cells. When an operator 'initiates', it
is assumed to instantaneously take a copy of its domain cells. When it
'terminates' it is assumed to instantaneously put values into its
range cells. Some models allow multiple initiations of an operator
without a corresponding termination between. This implies a first-in-

first-out buffer of domain cell values within the operator.

2.2.2   Control directed graph

This indicates the required ordering of data graph operations, and is designed to enforce that ordering. The graph consists of operators and cells, with the operators having directed arcs to and from the cells. Operators have a domain and a range of cells but these must be distinct, i.e. no control cell may be in the domain and range of the same control operator, but they are normally in the domain of one operator and the range of another (Fig. 2.2A).

It is here that the various models diverge slightly. In the basic model the control cells are counters and they are allowed to hold only non-negative integers. A control operator is said to be 'enabled' when all of its input cells contain positive integers. When it 'occurs', it decrements its input cells and increments its output cells. It is obvious that this model requires that no two control operators may 'occur' simultaneously, to prevent two operators attempting to change the same counter simultaneously (Fig. 2.2B). Some variations allow a cell to be in the input set of more than one operator. This requires the operator, for which it is in the output set, to increment it by more than one, and also gives problems with its succeeding operators not occurring an equal number of times. A further variation is the 'binary' model which IDES uses. The cells may only contain 0 or 1. This presents restrictions which are necessary for hardware and it also eases the analysis problems. A further modification (CASE and SARA) is to permit control operators to occur with the 'or' of the input control cells, i.e. if one cell is non-zero the operator can occur, and decrement that control cell. If two or more cells are non-zero then each one causes an occurrence, i.e. the 'conservative-or'. The basic model only has 'Ands'. Some models retain a semantic link with the originating Petri Net in that they describe the act of decrementing an input control cell and incrementing an output control cell to be the movement of a 'token' from the input to the output.

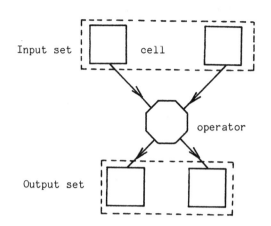

FIG. 2.2A.   Control operator and control cells

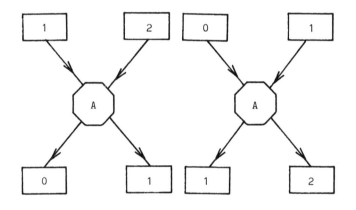

Enabled   --------->   Occurred

FIG. 2.2B.   Control cell changes when a control operator occurs

2.2.3 The relationship between control and data operators

Control operators and data operators are linked by corresponding names. For each data operator D, there is an initiate control operator D-i, and a terminate control operator D-t (Fig. 2.3). When the initiate operator D-i 'occurs', sometime after it is enabled, it simultaneously decrements its input counters and increments its output

16

counters, and passes an activation signal to the data operator which
causes it to 'read' its domain cells. At some later time the data
operator completes its operation and passes a 'done and ready-to-
write' signal to the termination control operator D-t. If the termination event is fully enabled, it occurs, decrementing its input
counters and incrementing its output counters, and a write of values
into the range data cells takes place. Some models allow multiple initiations without corresponding terminations. Usually the connections
to the data graph are implied and there is simply a counter between
D-i and D-t which is a count of the excess of initiates over terminates.

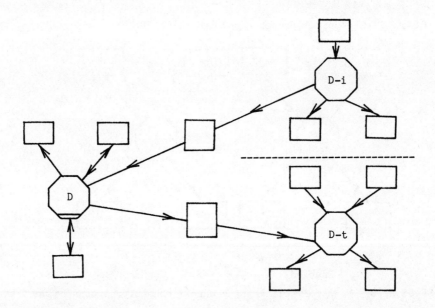

FIG. 2.3.   Relationship between control and data operators

Clearly some mechanism must exist for returning a value from the
data graph to the control graph to vary the control sequence depending
on data operation results. This may be represented by enabling different terminate operators for the operation, but is most easily dealt
with by adding to the set of control operators some whose sole func-

tion is to test data values and take decisions based on these values. The simplest one is a two-way branch on a value being true or false. Because of the diversity of the models, it is appropriate at this point to define the IDES model in more detail.

2.3   THE IDES DIRECTED GRAPH MODEL

2.3.1   The IDES model data-graph

The data-graph (DG) consists of directed arcs joining nodes representing data operators, data cells, and data busses. The IDES data operators and data cells (fig. 2.4) behave as previously described in Section 2.2.1. The data bus is a specifically hardware addition introduced to overcome some analytical problems caused when describing real hardware. It can be regarded as another type of data cell, except that it can only hold data while it is being continuously written to. Topologically, the only restrictions on the DG are that the arcs may only connect cells(busses) to operators or vice versa. Thus the DG can be cyclic or disconnected if required. All nodes in the DG are named, either because they are referenced from the control graph or for syntactic reasons in the language used to specify graphs, G.

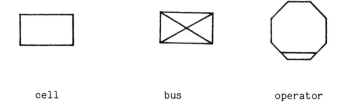

cell   bus   operator

FIG. 2.4.   IDES data graph symbols

2.3.2   The IDES model control-graph

The control graph (CG) is an acyclic directed graph with a unique Start node (the Blockhead, BH) and a unique End node (the Blockend,

BE). Every node in the CG must lie on a path (sequence of arcs) from the BH. Every node which is not in a subgraph (see below) must lie on a path to the BE. Nodes in the CG are either control cells or control operators. As in the DG, arcs may only connect cells to operators and vice versa. The IDES control operators are shown in Fig. 2.5. Because IDES uses the binary model, i.e. control cells may only contain 0 or 1, then the 'initiate' and 'terminate' control operators are combined into a single symbol, and the control cells are subsumed into the operator symbol on its input arcs. Thus a clearer, more easily understood control graph is produced. The 'And' operator of Fig. 2.5 shows this simplification of the representation. There are 4 types of control operator, all of which have a common initiation rule as follows:

When an operator has a one in each of its input cells and no ones in any of its output cells, it initiates, changing all of its input cells to zero.

The effect of firing depends on the type of the control operator. In the simplest case, the Syntax And, the action is 'place a one in each output cell'. Thus the Syntax And is merely a control flow synchronisation operator. Syntax Ands have no names and are not associated with any DG node.

The rule for the And operator is simply an extension of that for the Syntax And :

Initiate the corresponding data operator and, on receiving a termination signal, place a one in each of the output control cells.

The 'corresponding data operator' is the operator in the DG with the same name. Every named control operator has exactly one corresponding node in the DG. Clearly the Syntax And is degenerate and could simply be simulated by firing a null operator.

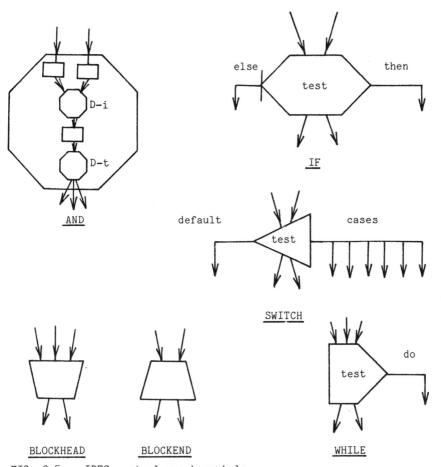

FIG. 2.5.   IDES control graph symbols

In order for the CG to represent realistic algorithms it must have a
capacity for making data-dependent branching decisions. The 'If',
'Switch' and 'While' operators implement this in various ways and are
generically known as Test operators. They have some properties in
common. Each has a name which refers to a DG cell or bus, rather than
an operator.   Each has one or more associated subgraphs. A subgraph
is either a single control operator or a set of connected operators
with a unique Start operator and a unique End operator. The start and
end, like BH and BE, have no function other than to arbitrate access

to the subgraph. They behave functionally like Syntax Ands. A sub-graph may be likened to a compound statement in a block-structured programming language. Entry to the subgraph can only be through the Start, and exit through the End. Thus nodes in the subgraph are iso-lated from the rest of the CG. A subgraph may contain nodes of any type, including those which possess further subgraphs. Every node in a subgraph must be on a path from the appropriate Start to the corresponding End. The DG has no subgraph as such, but of course sub-graph operators in the CG still reference the DG.

The If operator has two subgraphs, known as 'then' and 'else'. Its action on being initiated is:

> Test the value in the corresponding cell or bus. If it is 'true' place a one in the 'then' subgraph, otherwise place a one in the 'else' subgraph.

When control finds its way through to the end of the subgraph, ones are placed in the normal output cells of the If. The 'else' branch of the If may be omitted if desired but the 'then' branch must always be present.

The Switch operator has almost the same function, except that it can test non-binary values. It has a number (>1) of subgraphs, called cases, each with an associated value, and optionally one default sub-graph. One of the 'case' subgraphs is selected upon the basis of the corresponding DG value, or the 'default' if none of the case values match. The case values must all be different.

Finally, the While operator has one subgraph, called a 'do'. It provides the essential facility for iteration in the CG, since in all other respects the CG is acyclic. The action is:

> If the corresponding DG value is 'true', place a one in the 'do' subgraph. When the subgraph terminates, test the value

again and repeat. As soon as the test fails a one is placed in each of the while operators normal output cells.

The loop may be executed zero times. The 'do' branch may be omitted, giving the effect of simply waiting for the while to terminate (i.e for some condition to cease to apply).

2.4   THE BENEFITS OF THE DIRECTED GRAPH MODEL

There must be some benefit if this model is to be used, and is of use. One benefit is that the schema, i.e. the representation using the directed graph model, can be tested for its possession or otherwise of certain properties.

2.4.1   Losslessness

This is the property that every data operator can potentially change its output cells, i.e. it has a 'range'. This means that the data operator actually does something, and it would be surprising if any schema were to be drawn without this property.

2.4.2   Repetition freeness

It has been stated that every data operator must put the same values into its range cells if initiated with the same values in its domain cells. This is called a 'repetition'. A graph can be tested to establish 'repetition freeness', i.e. that between consecutive initiations of a data operator D, other operations occur which have the capability of changing the contents of the domain cells of the operator D. As the schema is uninterpreted, it cannot be said that the contents of the domain cells will in fact be altered. However, this property shows that the schema is finite-state, i.e. for nonbinary schema there is an upper bound for the value in each control cell (counter) and hence in the size of the first-in/first-out data buffer required within a data operator.

2.4.3   Persistence

This property states that once   an   event   is   enabled   to   occur,   it
remains   so   until it actually occurs. This property is automatic with
the IDES model.

2.4.4   Determinacy

This is the most valuable property which can be tested. The model   implies   that   unless the initiations and terminations of data operators
are specifically sequenced, then they may occur in any arbitrary   order.   A   schema   is determinate if the result of the computation, using
the same data, will give the same result every time,   irrespective   of
the   order   of initiation and termination of potentially parallel data
operations. There is no race hazard caused by   the   concurrency.   This
property   reduces to ensuring that one data operator cannot write to a
data cell which is able to be read by another data operator simultaneously   (the   reading   is sequenced to be always before or always after
the writing), and a data operator may not be enabled   to   write   to   a
data   cell   at   the same time that another data operator is enabled to
write to the same cell (there must be definite sequencing on these two
terminations).   As   a byproduct of the process of establishing whether
or not a particular schema is determinate, it is possible   to   manipulate a determinate control graph to possess the maximum parallelism in
it without violating the determinacy property.   This   results   in   the
maximally   parallel   version   of   the   graph.   Determinate graphs are
equivalent if they produce the same maximally parallel versions.   However, schema being equivalent does not mean that the corresponding algorithms are equivalent, because the schema are uninterpreted.

The problem of determinacy testing is the reason for one or two   aspects   of   the   IDES   model.   First, it does not have the 'or' control
operator because this permits the construction of loops in the control
graph, and makes the proof or otherwise of determinacy a mammoth problem for just a few nodes. This is because the reachability set of   the

graph (i.e. the number of different states it can attain) is so enormous that it cannot be analysed with reasonable resources. (The 'or' operator allows the equivalent of a 'goto'). However, the construction of loops within the graph must be possible, and the If, While and Switch operators, which test values in the data graph and branch or repeat accordingly, are used for this. It is the removal of gotos from the set of operators which permits easy analysis for determinacy, and is the same basis which makes structured (goto-less) programming such an improvement over unstructured programming.

2.4.5 Maximal parallelism

This is due to Bain [18] derived from a technique mentioned by Coffman and Denning [19]. It is a technique whereby a determinate graph can be processed in such a way that all operators which can be fired in parallel are so fired, while not violating determinacy. Thus all unnecessary sequentiality is removed from the graph, with a potential increase in performance. A graph so processed is called a maximally parallel control graph. It is discussed in detail in chapter 4.

2.4.6 Hierarchy

The final property to note about the directed graphs is that they can be made hierarchical. Clearly it is valuable to be able to analyse a part of the system, and, having established that it is 'correct' to forget about it as far as it affecting the rest of the system is concerned. Alternatively, it is valuable to design top down, and so be able to expand any node in a graph to an arbitrary number of levels, and at each level not have to consider levels above or below in the attempts to establish determinacy etc.

Hierarchical constructs are the reason for the blockhead and blockend operators. They enclose a pair of graphs and enable a control graph to be represented at the higher level by an And operator, and the data graph to be represented by a data operator attached to any cells which it reads from or writes to at the higher level (these data cells have lines at their top or bottom in the original graph).

Because it uses a binary model, IDES blocks can only be initiated once before terminating (there is a connection from the blockend to the blockhead to allow it to be reinitiated). This makes the representation of pipelines more difficult, but non-binary models can handle this more easily.

2.4.7   Concurrent processing

Whilst the model has been derived for the specification and design of concurrent hardware, it has some applications to software. The schema is very valuable in analysing concurrent processing algorithms for data flow computers, or other multiple-instruction/multiple-data (MIMD) multiprocessors, including multimicroprocessor systems. The maximum number of parallel streams in the control graph reveals the maximum number of processing elements which can be active at any one time during the execution of the algorithm. For an algorithm with a maximum of X parallel streams, then processing elements in excess of X do not provide any improvement in the execution time.

CHAPTER 3
IDES

3.1   INTRODUCTION TO IDES

The basic inspiration for the IDES system came from project LOGOS at
Case Western Reserve University under the direction of Professor
E.L. Glaser. [16]. Professor Glaser had been conscious for some
years of the need for an integrated design method for large computer
systems. He considered that software engineers needed software tools
which adhered to rigidly enforced standards and that the efforts of a
design team could best be integrated by a centralised on-line database. Such a database would be used for recording design decisions,
analysing the properties of a design and ensuring that all aspects of
it were fully and formally specified. In accordance with contemporary
ideas on structured programming, particularly with regard to operating
systems, it was decided that the representational system should be
modular and hierarchical in nature. The advantages of this approach
are well known:

1) Several designers can work independently on different parts
of the design. As long as the interfaces between modules are
well-defined the coordination of the component parts is relatively straightforward.

2) A module at some level in the system can call on modules at
lower levels to perform some function, without regard to how

that function is to be implemented. For example, in the case
of the T.H.E. operating system [20] programs at one level can
be regarded as working in the machine code of a virtual
machine at a lower level.

3) The correctness of a particular module depends only on the
interconnections between its components, assuming that each
component is itself correct. In short, modular hierarchical
systems provide a way to cope with complexity.

Having determined that their system would be structured it became
clear to the LOGOS team that, since the lowest levels of a computer
system comprise the actual hardware, it would be ideal if the
representation they chose would work equally well in hardware as in
software. If this were the case a computer system could be designed as
an integrated unit with the split between hardware and software being
postponed until the design was well-defined. The increasing use of microprogramming or firmware to implement instruction sets gave further
strength to this idea.

The remaining requirements for the representational system were that
it should be declarative and that it should be capable of expressing
parallelism. A declarative system is one which exhibits the structure
of the represented model rather than its function. Functional
representations are useful if the designer wants to express the external behaviour of a model, for example for simulation purposes. However, they cannot wholly take the place of a structural representation
since it is essentially a structure that is being designed, albeit
with functional constraints. The need to represent parallelism is fundamental for hardware design, but the team considered that it would be
useful in developing future software systems as well, since these are
liable to be highly concurrent. It was also thought that a suitable
representation system would allow automatic checking of duplicate
designs to avoid redundant effort, but little seems to have come of
this [21].

As stated in chapter 2, the representational system finally chosen by the LOGOS team was introduced by Karp and Miller [13]. They felt that this was the model that most nearly filled their requirements outlined above.

3.2   THE AIM OF THE IDES SYSTEM

The objective of providing a complete design environment means that no one language or representational system was likely to satisfy the need for different ways of looking at a target system. The original LOGOS workers at Case Western had envisaged hardware being directly implemented from LOGOS graphs. At Heriot-Watt, Howard [22] and Manugian [23] had designed hardware modules which functioned in the manner specified for control operators in the Binary Model. However, the IDES team took the view that, while the graph model had several attractive features as a vehicle for an algorithmic specification of a digital system, it was not necessarily desirable to implement the control graph directly in hardware. The original LOGOS graph specification was thus modified by the IDES team to form a new structured graph model represented by IDES graphs. This meant that IDES had to have at least two levels or stages, one for the algorithmic specification of a system and the other for its eventual realisation. It soon became clear that an intermediate stage would be advantageous, to convert between these two disparate representations. Accordingly, the following three-level scheme was proposed:

1) Level 1, the ARCHITECTURE Level: IDES graphs formally specify the algorithm to be implemented. A modification of the structured model is used. The hierarchy of graphs ends in a set of bottom-level graphs which contain primitive data operators.

2) Level 2, the IMPLEMENTATION Level: From the graphs of Level 1 are constructed modules in a Hardware Description Language (HDL). IDES data operators which are not of a recog-

nised primitive type may be input directly by the designer. The set of HDL descriptions forms the specification of a register transfer machine.

3) Level 3, the REALISATION Level: The HDL from Level 2 is used to construct lists of parts and their interconnections. Interactive design programs refer to a library of existing chips to produce a circuit specification in terms of available components. The library is kept current by the use of a chip compiler to add new devices to the repertoire.

These three levels will be described in more detail in subsequent sections. An overall block diagram of the IDES system is shown in figure 3.1.

Although it is envisaged that most design done on the IDES system would proceed in the top-down manner suggested above, it is entirely possible for a designer to use a facility at one level without being compelled to take his design through previous levels. To this end, each level can be entered directly via text files, which may equally well be created by a design system program or by a human user. For example, it is possible that, with simple designs, some users might wish to omit the Level 1 graph stage but would describe their ideas directly in the Level 2 HDL. By the same token, even if the HDL description is produced by the Implementation software, there is nothing to prevent the user from modifying it if he thinks he can make improvements. This accords well with the precepts of the Ideal System in that the levels are connected but are usable independently. The use of text files for inter-level communication also means that the various parts of the IDES system could be developed in isolation and rigorously tested with hand-generated input. This textual interface between levels would need to be removed from a production version of the IDES system in the interests of efficiency.

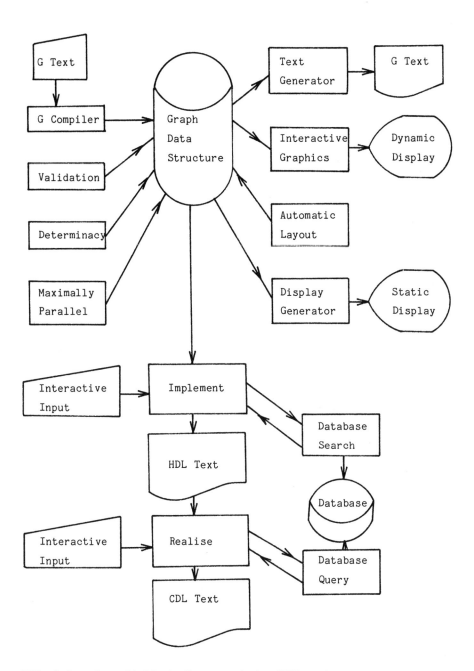

FIG. 3.1.   Overall block diagram of the IDES system

One possible criticism might be that the graph model was designed for asynchronous operation, whereas most present-day digital systems use some form of synchronous logic. If the IDES graphs were to be implemented directly this may be a valid point, although VLSI systems are now requiring self-timed logic because of the effect of cross-chip transmission delays. However, it should be remembered that they are being used purely as an expressive device for representing the parallel structure of hardware algorithms in a manner amenable to uninterpreted analysis. The eventual implementation of the control graph may be synchronous, or asynchronous, without affecting the validity of the model provided that, in the synchronous case, care is taken to provide sufficient delays between clock pulses. The design programs at Level 3 are intended to supply this check, since there is obviously a close dependency on actual hardware.

Although the IDES graphs themselves do not appear except at Level 1, they make their presence felt at lower levels. The basic architectural structure of the design is defined at Level 1 and carried through the whole process. This means that the distinction between control and data is preserved, and that the hierarchical form of the Level 1 specification influences the eventual manner of implementation. With regard to the latter point it might give rise to one of the stock arguments against Structured Programming, namely that it is inefficient. There is no reason why this should be a severe problem in most cases. If the result of a design attempt is not satisfactory, the designer will revise his original specification and try again. As indicated above, he is not constrained to accept what IDES produces at each stage. However, it is better practice to modify the original Level 1 design and thereby improve the result. It seems, from initial designs, that most descriptions will not cover more than two or three sublevels within the graph hierarchy, so it is likely that the potential inefficiencies this might produce, in the form of redundant components, would be outweighed by the advantages of a modular, understandable, and modifiable design. However, duplication of components need not always be undesirable. It may actually be desirable in order to achieve a maximally parallel system, and hence optimise thröughput.

Ideally, there should be some way of optionally post-processing a design, possibly at Level 2, with a view to minimising the component count. This would entail incorporating the entire set of modules to be optimised into a single HDL description and examining it for redundancies in much the same manner as a compiler might use an extra pass through the object code to do peep-hole optimisations. There are no immediate plans to do this.

3.3 THE IDES SYSTEM

Before discussing the three levels of IDES in more detail it will be appropriate to place the research project in context by outlining the computing environment.

The computing facility consists of a PDP11/45 mini-computer, running the UNIX time-sharing operating system from Bell Laboratories. [24]. The capability that the user may run several processes concurrently and the mechanism for process intercommunication, known as a pipe, have proved very useful in the IDES project. The decision to make full use of UNIX facilities, including writing all IDES software in the UNIX high-level language C [25] means that the resulting system is not readily transportable to a non-UNIX site. Once again, it should be emphasised that what has been undertaken is a research exercise intended to test the ideas incorporated in the proposed system. Reference to UNIX features will be made as appropriate.

3.3.1 The architecture level

At this, the top level of the system, the main area of work has been the adaptation of the original LOGOS directed-graph model to make it more suitable for hardware design, and the specification and implementation of a special graph language [26] to allow its description. Auxiliary software has been written to provide a complete language system for integration into the design suite.

The motivation for a graph input language is that the method used in previous LOGOS systems, computer graphics, was considered to have certain disadvantages. Graphics input, although a natural mode of expression for non-linear structure, is often restricted by the amount of detail which can fit on a display screen. Ideally it should be used to edit a previously specified picture rather than to draw one from scratch. This means that most directed-graph input can be done via the normal text editor, with the graphics display being used only occasionally. The IDES system therefore allows either mode to be used interchangeably, communication being achieved through the common data structure.

Since the full Graphics Editor has yet to be developed, a preliminary Display program has been written to allow graph structures to be shown without interaction. A companion program, Layout, takes a graph data structure and attempts to supply co-ordinate values for the nodes of the graph in order to produce a reasonable picture for Display to show. The Layout program will, of course, still be needed in transferring from text to graphics even after the Graphics Editor is written, in order to provide an initial picture for the user to work on. The language itself, known as G, is the subject of chapter 4 and will only be given a cursory treatment at this point.

The example shown in figure 3.2 describes a simple 16 bit shift-and-add multiplier named 'mul' which takes inputs 'multip' and 'multic' and generates an output called 'result'. The body of the description begins with the declaration of cells to be used in the data graph i.e. count, carry, const, a, b & out. Following this we have the specification of the operators used in the data graph and their interconnections. The keyword 'type' introduces a name for a data operator of which there may be many instances. In line 7 of the description a data operator called 'initcount' is declared. This is of type 'transfer'. It takes as input the data cell 'const' and writes to the data cell 'count'. The specification of the control graph follows that of the data graph and consists of a set of chains. Each control operator refers to the data operator of the same name. The symbols '<' and '>' refer respectively to the start and the end of the control flow. The control graph may be interpreted as:

> Upon activation(i.e. at the 'start') do 'inita'. When this is complete do 'initb'. Follow this with 'initcount' and then 'initout'. While the data cell 'count' holds data (is non-zero) do repeatedly the operations specified in the subgraph (line 16) and then do the operation 'loadres'.

```
mul(multip,multic:result)
{
        dcell count,carry;
        dcell const;
        dcell a,b,out;

        type transfer   initcount(const:count),
                         inita(multip:a),initb(multic:b),
                         loadres(out:result);
        type shiftl      shiftout(:out),shifta(:a);
        type dec         deccnt(:count);
        type clear       initout(:out);
        self             add(b,out:out),tstc(a:carry);

        <:inita:initb:initcount:initout:while count do  {
                <:shiftout:shifta:tstc:if carry then add :deccnt:>;
        }:loadres:>;
}
```

FIG. 3.2   Multiplier expressed in G

In order to assist comprehension, the graph pair is drawn in figure 3.3, using the IDES graphical symbols defined in chapter 2.

Programs written in the level 1 language are compiled to produce the data structure files for single control-graph data-graph pairs. Several supplementary programs may then examine the structures produced. The G compiler is deliberately loose in the specifications it will accept, confining itself mainly to checking the syntax of the G program. There are a number of reasons for this. Firstly, it was thought desirable for the compiler to be single pass and hence fairly fast. Secondly, because the text is specifying a two-dimensional graph structure it is quite easy to make semantic errors and yet rather difficult for the user to spot them when they occur in text. Typical errors might be caused by a redundant path between two control nodes, or by a cycle in the control graph. The Layout program must be able to accept even such invalid structures and allow them to be displayed, making debugging an easier task, so the compiler will produce a data structure file even in cases where it could quite easily have detected errors. Thirdly, any checks built into the compiler would have to be duplicated by the Graphics Editor, giving rise to a potent source of error and incompatibility between the two forms. The verification of semantic correctness is therefore carried out upon the data structure file itself, irrespective of where it came from, by a program called Valid. This modularity also allows for any future changes in the definition of 'validity' to be easily and quickly incorporated.

By a similar argument, determinacy of a graph is checked by another program, Determ, using a modification of Bain's algorithm [27]. One of the entries in the data structure is a 'status' word which indicates which programs have already operated upon it. Thus the Determ program, for example, will refuse to certify a graph as determinate unless it has previously been approved by Valid.

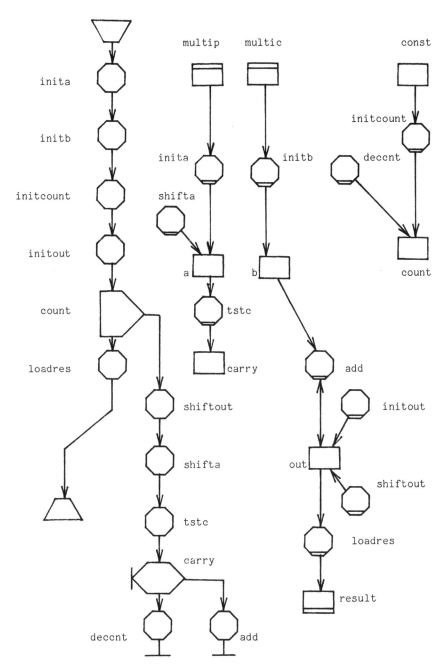

FIG. 3.3.   Graphs of the multiplier of figure 3.2

One further facility available at this level of the system involves the transformation of the control graph in order to improve its performance. The procedure is to examine the control graph for nodes which operate in sequence but which have no potentially conflicting data cells in common. Such nodes can just as validly operate in parallel, thus removing unnecessary sequentiality. The result of reforming the control graph in this way yields a maximally parallel but functionally equivalent version. The reformed, maximally parallel, control graph of the multiplier example is shown in figure 3.4.

For completeness, there is also an uncompiler, called Tx. This takes a graph data structure file and reconstructs the original G text. It might be used if the original source was accidentally lost, but is really intended to do for text what Layout does for graphics. In other words, if the user has created his structure or edited it via the Graphics Editor, he is at liberty to convert it back into G form for perusal. Since a text editor is often more convenient than a display screen for adding detailed information or comments this is a valuable option. The text form generally would be more suitable for communication with other designers than the data structure, and allows more convenient publication and documentation.

3.3.2 The implementation level

All the IDES models are hierarchical in nature. That is to say, they may be regarded as indefinitely, though non-recursively, nested. A graph at one level is defined in terms of graphs at lower levels and may itself appear as a single node at a higher level. It is convenient to think of this nesting as being achieved through the expansion of operators in the data graph. This concept plays an important part in the design of the G language. More immediately, it means that a graph hierarchy will be interactively transformed by the Implementation software into a hierarchy of data-transforming register transfer machines, each with its associated control (chapter 5). Since the graph structure is essentially uninterpreted, how is this to be done?

Clearly, a realistic design cannot allow the graph hierarchy to be infinitely nested. At some point there must be a bottom—level which is not further defined in terms of other graphs. It is this level which provides the interface to the Realisation program. The method of achieving this is as follows:

> Each bottom—level graph in a design is examined for the types of its data operators. Certain types of operator will be immediately recognised by the Implementation program as being primitive. Those which are not primitive, if any, may have been defined by the IDES user either as further levels in the graph hierarchy or as HDL descriptions. In either case, this leads eventually to a complete definition in terms of primitives. Alternatively, the designer may decide that he wants to use a particular component not recognised as a primitive by the Level 2 software, but without defining it as an HDL program. The HDL allows him to do so, simply passing the information on to Level 3, where the new component has presumably been properly entered in the chip library. The set of primitives, undefined components, and HDL descriptions is then used to construct an HDL description of the bottom—level graph and the process is repeated for each bottom—level graph in the design. Higher level graphs are then treated in order, incorporating the HDL descriptions already produced as subcircuits. The hierarchy of graphs is thus transformed into a hierarchy of register-transfer machines.

The break between using Level 1 and 2 descriptions is entirely at the designer's discretion. The Level 2 software is biased towards graph structures expressed in terms of recognised primitives, but their use is not compulsory. The key property of HDL programs is that they reflect hardware much more closely than do G programs. The structural rules for IDES graphs, necessary in order to allow formal analysis, occasionally limit their usefulness for directly modelling hardware. The designer may balance his choice of representation

between the advantages of rigorous analysis on the one hand and more
direct control over the end result on the other.

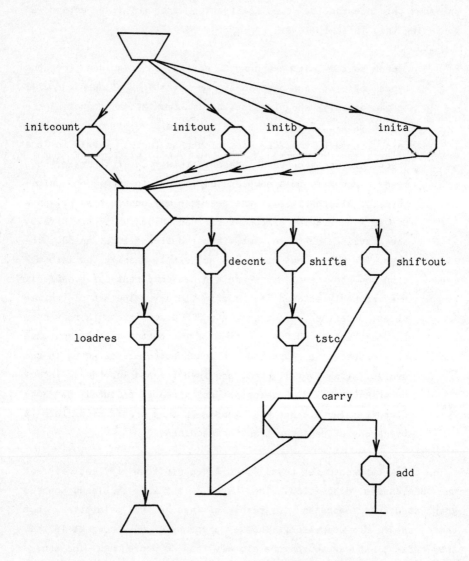

FIG. 3.4 Maximally parallel multiplier control graph

The HDL must deal in the physical sizes of components, such as the

number of bits in a register or words in a memory, since every object
in an HDL description will eventually have a hardware counterpart at
Level 3. In a similar manner to a level 1 G description the body of
an HDL description starts with a declaration section which gives not
only the type of an entity but its width in bits, the number of elements if relevant, and perhaps certain features which must be present:

```
register              a<8>;
memory                scratch[7]<8>;
counter(binary,up,down) stc<3>;
```

The section of a description corresponding to a G data graph consists
of the various connections between declared objects and is termed the
transfers section. This section allows a variety of transfer types:

1) Simple Transfers specify the ordered (bitwise) connection
of an output port on an object to an input port on a second
object:

```
a.out<1,3-5,9> -> b.in<0,2,5-7>;
```

If no bits at all are specified in either the source or sink
of a transfer then it is assumed that the connection applies
across the full width of the port concerned. Similarly if
there is only one input(output) port on an object then the
name of the sink(source) port may be omitted:

```
a -> b;
```

specifies a connection of all the bits of the single output
port of 'a' to the bits of the single input port of 'b'.

2) Loads are used to specify the transfer of a constant value
to a particular port or to a set of bits in that port:

```
32 -> b.in<0-4>;
```

Bits within the specified range which are not asserted in order to load the number will be actively de-asserted. Bits outwith the range of the transfer will be left untouched. A binary load is also allowed:

```
1,0,1,1,0 -> b.in<0-4>;
```

This form allows the specific assertion or de-assertion of bits in a port.

3) Assertions do not call for the transfer of data between objects but are manipulative operations on them:

```
r0.inc;
```

means assert the increment function on register r0. The function associated with this may be a complex operation involving many individual pins and/or ports depending on its chip data base definition.

4) Tests are used to provide a data-dependent branching facility in the control flow. At present tests are implemented as bit-wise or's of a particular data-cell or a subset of its bits:

```
a.in<0,3-6,9>;
```

In this case the test is considered 'true' if any of the bits 0,3,4,5,6,9 are 'true'. Alternatively, tests may be expressed using a complex boolean expression involving a number of ports on a variety of objects:

```
a.out<0> | b.out<8> & a.out<8>
```

Transfers may have a name associated with them (named transfer):

```
cgeno == cycle<0-3> -> idbus<0-3>;
```

as in this case, where the transfer of bits 0 to 3 of 'cycle' to
'idbus' is given the name 'cgeno'. In this case the transfer is considered switchable, the connection only being made active at one or
more particular point(s) in the control sequence. Unnamed (permanent)
transfers are non-switchable and the objects concerned are permanently
connected.

The final section of an HDL description is the control graph and
this has basically the same form as a level 1 G description.

It can be seen that the translation from an IDES data graph into HDL
is largely a question of replacing one structure with its dual. In the
level 1 case, the control graph initiates operations (nodes) which
read inputs and write outputs, whereas in level 2 the control initiates transfers (arcs) between devices. An example of the HDL form
is given in figure 3.5 where the multiplier used as an example for
level 1 has been automatically converted using the implementation programs.

It should be noted that at level 2 there is no distinction between
'data operators' and 'data cells', and consequently no topological
restriction on the interconnections which may be made. This opens up
the possibility of quite drastic changes in the form of the 'data
graph' taking place in the interests of efficiency. For example, in
level 1 a memory would usually be represented as an operator which,
upon being requested to Read, transformed the contents of its associated MAR (Memory Address Register) to data in its MDR (Memory Data Register). Although the MAR and MDR do physically exist they might not
be independent of the memory itself, and so the set of one operator
and two cells could be replaced by a single component. The inverse
case might also occur if the designer requested an operation which was

not available as a single component but had to be constructed from existing parts. The algorithms to perform this kind of intelligent
matching automatically may well be beyond present day techniques, but
the ability to intervene by hand if necessary is sufficient at
present. A more detailed specification of the HDL and Implement can
be found in chapter 5.

```
mul(multip<16>,multic<16>:result<32>) {
        register carry<1>,b<16>;
        register(dec)    count<5>;
        register(shiftl)         a<16>;
        register(clear,shiftl)  out<32>;
        self tstc,add;
/* Data Graph */
        a -> tstc.I[1];
        b -> add.I[1];
        out -> add.I[2];

        loadres == out -> .result;
        initb == .multic -> b;
        inita == .multip -> a;
        initcount == 0 -> count;

        tstc == tstc.O[1] -> carry;
        add == add.O[1] -> out;

        shifta == a.shiftl;
        shiftout == out.shiftl;
        decent == count.dec;
        initout == out.clear;

        count =b= count<0>|count<1>|count<2>|count<3>|count<4>;
        carry =b= carry<0>;
```

```
/* Control Graph */
        <: initout,initcount,initb,inita;
        initout: while(count) do {
                <: deccnt,shifta,shiftout;
                deccnt: >;
                shifta: tstc;
                tstc: if(carry) then {
                        <: add;
                        add: >;
                };
                carry: >;
                shiftout: carry;
        };
        count: loadres;
        loadres: >;
        initcount: count;
        initb: count;
        inita: count;
}
```

FIG. 3.5.   Maximally parallel multiplier implemented in HDL

3.3.3   The realisation level

In contrast with Levels 1 and 2, which provide opportunities for the
designer to experiment with different approaches to his target system,
Level 3 is intended to aid him in selecting the physical components
with which the final design will be implemented. Operation of the
Realisation software is therefore interactive, but automatic facilities are available to take care of the well-understood but tedious detail of circuit design (e.g. generating a 32-bit register from 4-bit
registers). In accordance with the IDES philosophy, none of these facilities are to be forced on the user, who can intervene by hand. However, it is foreseen that one of the more valuable results of using
Level 3, instead of realising designs entirely by hand, will be the

constant checking done by the software on the 'legality' of the designer's proposals, particularly with regard to circuit enabling and connection consistency.

In the normal course of events entry to Level 3 will be via the HDL descriptions produced at the Implementation Level. In transforming these into circuit specifications the following steps must be taken:

1) Syntactic and Semantic checking of the input description. It is at this stage that an HDL description is checked for a variety of simple errors: the use, in a transfer, of an undeclared object, the inconsistency of bits in a transfer etc. In general any errors which would make it difficult to construct the internal data structure used by the program to represent the design, are checked.

2) Forming the undefined bit widths of ports and setting up 'full width' transfers. Having correctly parsed the input and created an internal representation, consistency checking of all the transfers to and from a particular port can take place and any default situations taken care of. It is possible that across all the transfers in the description only two bits in a particular 4 bit port are used. What is to be done with the remaining bits? The answer is obviously dependent upon the type of port (input, output, function etc.) and what types of transfer are involved. If, for example, the transfer is the load of a constant, then all the bits in the port should be actively asserted or de-asserted. Conversely should the transfer be the assertion of certain function bits then the remaining bits in the port can often assume their 'don't care' values.

3) Allocating a component or set of components to each object in the HDL 'data graph'. For each object which has not been specifically named then a search must be made of the database

to find a suitable component(s). The search itself takes the form of an iterative search, check, select loop utilising the database Search and Query programs. Initially, the search is based upon specific attributes given at declaration time:

counter(binary,down)   count<5>;

would give rise to a search expression:

counter & binary & bit=5

This failing to produce an answer the realisation program goes through a repertoire which gradually expands the search pattern, for example by asking for a counter with greater than five bits and eventually, all else failing, looking for a counter which although itself has a bit width less than 5 has a known expansion algorithm. At any time if a 'suitable' chip is encountered then the checkout procedure is carried out. This involves using the database Query program to ask for specific information about the chip: does it have all the ports required and are they of the required width, can it support all the assertions which are required of it etc. If, as a result of these procedures, a set of possible chips is found, then assuming the designer has opted for it, a period of interaction takes place in which the 'best' chip for the job is chosen. Interaction being turned off, the realisation program will make the choice based upon some criterion that has been nominated for optimisation(cost, speed ...).

4) Specifying the detailed connections between the components in the design. This involves the expansion of transfers to an object which it has been decided must be realised as a set of circuits, into a set of similar transfers to the individual circuits:

```
        0256 -> x.in;
```

in this case the transfer of the octal constant 256 to x where
x is an 8 bit register (the IDES system maintains the convention of interpreting a leading zero to mean an octal number).
If x were to be realised using two 4 bit circuits then the
transfer must be converted internally to be of the form:

```
        016 -> x(circuit1).in;
        012 -> x(circuit2).in;
```

The manipulations required when the transfer is   truly
transferring data from one object to another and both of these
objects are to be realised as multiple circuits become quite
involved. A detailed description of them is to be found in
chapter 6. Having done this, transfers, which up to this
point have been between bits in ports, must now be converted
to represent connections between pins on packages or pads on
masks. The data graph has now been totally converted to
hardware and it is possible to take care of situations meaningful only at this 'absolute' level - unused pins on packages
are given the appropriate default conditions (held high or
low), transfers to ports which are busses are flagged to be
tri-state(say), power and clock pins are attended to etc.   A
whole host of normally manual, tedious tasks are carried out
at this stage.

5) Using the data graph realisation and the HDL description of
the control graph to design a controller for the target system.

The language used to represent the realisation of the design, the
Circuit Description Language (CDL), is not expected to be used as an
input media for a designer and is simply used as a textual interface
between realisation and a variety of programs (e.g. wiring list gen-

eration). As such, little will be said about it here except to say
that CDL is essentially a set of boolean equations representing the
gating required to make all the connections to each individual pin in
the circuit. This vehicle was used since it was seen to be useful for
the generation of logic diagrams and for the manual checking of a circuit.

3.3.4 The chip database

The central feature of the Realisation system is a database of chip or
circuit descriptions [28] which can be updated from manufacturers' ca-
talogues. Chips are formally specified, in a manner outlined below,
and input to the Chip Compiler. This produces two forms of output. The
first is a semi-compiled form of the chip description. It becomes part
of the database proper, and is used by the database Query program.
The second output is an entry in an Attributes File, which describes
the coarse properties of the chip (e.g. that it is a 4-bit low-power
Schottky latch) and points into the database where the detailed information is stored. This Attributes File allows the designer to search
efficiently for devices corresponding to given constraints using the
Query System software described in appendix IV.

Each data graph expressed in the Level 2 HDL may be regarded as a
set of black boxes connected by data paths. At Level 3 black boxes
may represent chips, logic elements or completed sub-designs. Data
paths are connected to black boxes via data ports, of which there are
three kinds: Input, Output and Address, denoted I, O and A respectively. Each black box (representing an ALU for example) may also have a
Function port, denoted F. The data paths may be individually labelled
by analogy with the HDL transfer operators. Only certain types of
transfer are allowed: O to A, O to I and O to F. The port naming convention was introduced to allow a systematic representation of complex
black boxes i.e. those which are not single chips.

The description of a chip is composed of a number of parts as follows:

1) The chip number is the chip's official designation   in   the
manufacturer's   catalogue (e.g. SN74153). A notational convention may be used for the chip number to   compress   information
about   a family of otherwise identical chips which have a wide
spectrum of   speed/power   characteristics: SN7400[0,LS,L,S,H]
refers to SN7400, SN74LS00, SN74L00, SN74S00 and SN74H00 where
all these chips may share the same data file.

2) Pin names give the association between catalogue names, pin
numbers and port designations e.g.

          PIN 3 = d4, I[1]<4> ;

indicates that the catalogue name of pin number 3 on the   chip
is 'd4' and it is bit 4 of input port 1 on the chip. If a port
designation is not given then a power supply name can be   used
(Vcc or Gnd) or the pin may be declared NC (Not Connected).

3) Macros are boolean expressions made up of   catalogue   names
or other macros:

          Load = !load & Clock & Enable ;   (1)
          Clock = +ck ;   (2)
          Enable = !p & !t ;   (3)

The names Load, Clock and Enable are macro names.   The   phrase
'+ck' in   line (2) means that the 'ck' pin on the chip (which
is probably the clock pin) is fired on a rising edge. The symbols   '!'   and   '&'   refer   to   the boolean COMPLEMENT and AND
operations respectively. Thus the Load macro means 'the   load,
p and t pins are low and the ck pin receives a rising edge'.

4) Port operations must be associated with every port. When   a

data transfer is fired the operations on the relevant ports
are automatically invoked:

PORT I[1]<4> = Load ;

means that the conditions specified by the macro Load must be
true when Input port 1 is used. The '<4>' declares the total
number of pins associated with that port.

5) Chip operations provide for conditions to be specified
under which the use of a port, pin or macro is legitimate:

Right = Sr & Clock : VALID = I[2] & !m ;

Macro 'Right' should only be enabled when data is connected to
port I[2] and pin 'm' is low. Similar keywords may be used to
specify the conditions under which a port, pin or macro can,
where appropriate, be changed, overridden or initialised
(CHANGE, OVERRIDE, INITIAL). The description may also indicate
that a port, pin or macro may be activated only after a given
event (WAIT), that there is a delay before an output changes
(DELAY), that a pin is open-collector or tri-state (OC or
TRI), that a port or pin has a certain fanin or fanout (FANIN
or FANOUT) and that a total circuit has a given maximum speed
(SPEED). If not specified, the values of SPEED, DELAY, FANIN
and FANOUT default to standard values.

6) Port expansion is a useful feature when the designer wishes
to produce a circuit built from many chips of the same type:

```
EXPAND =
{
        MODULO  I[1],O[1];
        COMMON clear, clock, F[1] ;
```

50

```
                    LSC.O[1]<MSB> -> MSC.I[3]<0> ;
                    MSC.O[1]<LSB> -> LSC.I[2]<0> ;

          }
```

This specifies how a 4 bit bidirectional shift register can be
replicated to make a 4n-bit equivalent. The data ports I[1]
and O[1] are expanded by the modulus of their width to give
Input and Output data ports of the width required. The keywords MSC, LSC, MSB and LSB stand for Most/Least Significant
Chip/Bit.

The Chip description software also allows a great deal of detail in
the specification of clocks and signal types which it would be super-
fluous to introduce here. A complete description of this is to be
found in chapter 6.

3.4   SUMMARY

The IDES system as described briefly is operational with the exception
of the interactive graphics module. The information for producing a
wiring list is completely contained in the CDL text of the design and
it could be extracted readily. In any event, wiring schedules would
not be needed if the system were to be adapted for the design of integrated circuits themselves, a metallisation mask generator being required.

It should be borne in mind that the software has been designed in a
modular manner, thus allowing the overall system to be developed
quickly, and be as flexible as possible. This reduced the man-hours
required, and enabled modifications to be made rapidly. As may be expected, this results in an adverse trade-off against the speed of execution of the design system, but this is logical in a research environment. The multiplier of figure 3.2 requires 6 minutes for its
complete design, while the design of an 8-bit microprocessor has taken
30 minutes. Rewriting the system, and using a bigger computer, would

reduce these times by an order of magnitude.

The following chapters introduce more detail on selected aspects of
the IDES system and expand on the brief overview contained in this
chapter.

CHAPTER 4

Algorithmic Hardware Descriptions

4.1 PHILOSOPHY

4.1.1 Introduction

The overall IDES computer-aided digital design system has been described in chapter 3. Briefly, the system is an attempt to integrate several different aspects of digital design by allowing the description of computer systems to be carried out at three conceptual levels of detail, known as the Architecture, Implementation and Realisation Levels respectively. The Implementation and Realisation Levels will be described in subsequent chapters. They are concerned with the progressively more detailed and device-oriented design of digital systems. The Architecture Level, the subject of this chapter, deals with a more abstract view of computations which is none the less geared to providing the other two Levels with a useful base on which to build a design.

The purpose of developing a formal model is to allow the description of 'computational systems' independently of their eventual implementation. Such an abstraction has as its primary task the specification of the control flow and data flow in the target system (i.e the computational system being designed). It describes the structure of an algorithm rather than its function. Such a formalism has several advantages:

1. The model of the target system can be analysed for properties, such as determinacy, which are a feature of the topology of the system independent of the detailed function of its components.

2. There is no commitment to any particular technology or basic set of devices. Even the designer's intention that the result will be a binary computer is at this stage irrelevant detail.

3. It is possible to provide a good set of control structures - similar to those advanced by structured programming enthusiasts - without worrying about the efficiency of their implementation.

4. As a corollary to the above, a formal method can enforce discipline on the user, encouraging good design practice. This could be especially important in teaching design to undergraduate engineers.

Other potential advantages of a widespread use of some formal design methodology include intercommunication between members of a design team, the possibility of determining for copyright purposes whether two designs are equivalent, the benefits of a central library of verified designs and so on.

In short, a formal structural model can provide for the hardware designer some of the advantages a high level language confers on the software engineer. What is missing at this stage is a functional description of what the target system is intended to do. In IDES, this is provided at lower levels in the design process.

4.1.2 Describing directed graph pairs with text

There are several reasons why the textual description of a directed graph pair is different from a conventional computer program. The language form used is therefore unlike a programming language although, as will be seen, there is an attempt to emphasise similarities where they exist. The major differences are:

1) The language must be capable of representing fully parallel structures with the same degree of generality as a diagram.

2) Since there are no interpreted operations no code can be produced to execute them.

3) The hierarchy of graph pairs is not the same as a subroutine calling structure in conventional software.

4) There is no global or common data.

In short, while a normal programming language may be compiled and executed in order to implement an algorithm, the graph language is used only for describing the structure of hardware algorithms expressed according to the IDES graph model. The above points will now be taken individually.

4.1.3 Parallelism

The representation of parallelism in programming languages has received scant attention from language designers. This is largely because most languages are intended for use on single processor machines (although it could also be argued that most machines have a single processor because software techniques have yet to be devised to cope adequately with parallelism). The usual method of specifying parallelism may be exemplified by the following Algol 68 fragment:

```
begin
        [100] int buffer;
        int inp = 0, outp = 0;
```

```
            sema used = level 0, unused = level 100;
            par ( do down unused;                         (a)
                   inp modab 100 plusab 1;
                   read(buffer[inp]);
                   up used
            od ,                                          (b)
            do down used;                                 (c)
                   outp modab 100 plusab 1;
                   print(buffer[outp]);
                   up unused
            od )                                          (d)
      end
```

As can be seen, this implements the well known 'readers and writers' problem. The two parallel processes are introduced in line (a). One runs from line (a) to line (b) and the other from line (c) to line (d). The keyword 'par' simply causes a set of processes to be 'collaterally elaborated' (executed in parallel). All the processes must finish before control leaves the 'par' block. This simple structure may be termed 'fork-and-join' parallelism, by analogy with a similar mechanism in PL/1. Essentially the same technique is used in the hardware design systems examined. For example, in ISP parallel actions are represented thus:

```
      IR <- M[Pc] ; Pc <- Pc+1 NEXT
```

where the NEXT causes a 'join' of all parallel activity at that context level before the next statement is executed. Some languages allow the nesting of parallel blocks according to the following (informal) syntax:

```
      par_block:      statement
            or        sequence of par_blocks
            or        list of par_blocks
```

where 'sequence' implies consecutive and 'list' parallel execution. This however would defeat the purpose of the fully asynchronous IDES model and would obscure the essential structure. Fork-and-join methods of representing parallelism are thus inadequate for the graph language.

A second mechanism for utilising non-linear structure is exemplified by the PL/1 ON condition and the APDL 'if ever' statement. These, however, were invented to deal with hardware traps and exceptions and are not suitable for IDES type synchronisation since they implicitly require a continuous test on whether the designated condition is true.

4.1.4   Uninterpreted data operations

The notion that data operators are uninterpreted is fundamental to the model. Nevertheless, it was tempting to consider the introduction of certain primitive operations in terms of which other operators (higher level graphs) could be defined. Such a step would not harm the formalism of the model but might make it easier to understand. However, the following objections were sufficient to cause the idea to be rejected:

1) The purpose of the Architecture Level is to present the abstract structure of an algorithm, not its function. Interpretation of what the structure represents is dependent on the designer and should not be biased by features wired into the language.

2) It would be highly impractical to offer a sufficiently complete set of primitive functions to suit every eventuality. Inevitably a user would some day want a function which was not in the primitive set but was available as a single piece of hardware. Since the communication between Levels 1 and 2 is via the lowest sub-level of the graph hierarchy he would be unable to avoid the problem by specifying the new function in

terms of the primitives without at the same time sacrificing the intended implementation as a single component.

3) All data operations must be explicitly named because of the cross-referencing convention between control graph and data graph. That is, if there are two adders, say, in the data graph, they must each have a distinguishing name and the names must be declared to be of type 'adder'. The introduction of special symbols for primitive operators would confuse the syntax rather than clarify it.

4) The aim of the graph language is not to produce executing code so there is no advantage to be gained from recognising certain operations as primitive.

In the event, of course, the algorithmic structure represented by the graph language must find expression as a hardware implementation, so interpretation must at some point be attached to it. This is done by the IDES level 2 (implementation) and level 3 (realisation) software.

4.1.5 The graph hierarchy

At first glance there is a strong resemblance between the hierarchy of graphs and the nesting of procedure calls in a block-structured programming language. The similarity, due to the common technique of structuring a problem to reduce its apparent complexity is, however, superficial. In the first place, the nesting of the graphs is entirely static. Storage is not dynamically allocated on entry to a sub-level graph or reclaimed on exit by any kind of run-time stack mechanism. It is all declared at compile time and exists throughout the lifetime of a given design. This has two principal consequences:

1) A design may not be recursive. Recursion requires the use of a dynamic stack to implement it and is not a meaningful

concept in hardware. For example, it is impossible to make a microprocessor, one of the components of which is an identical microprocessor.

2) Data cells retain their contents from one activation of a graph to the next. They are not re-initialised on each occasion. Again this reflects the realities of hardware where the contents of a memory cell do not normally change unless the cell is specifically written to.

Each graph may be regarded as a model of an algorithm which will eventually become a piece of hardware. This leads to the second disparity between sub-level graphs and software procedures. In a conventional program a particular function may be assigned to a subroutine and used repeatedly throughout the program in many different contexts. In hardware, however, it would be necessary to declare several different operators which were functionally identical. For example, a designer might call for a data graph containing two 'xyz' operators. This is not the same as calling an 'xyz' function twice because:

1) The two operators might be active in parallel.

2) They might have different inputs and/or outputs connected to them.

3) Their internal data cells would preserve information from one 'call' to the next, as described above.

It is thus possible for a graph to employ multiple identical sub-level graphs. Clearly they must all have different names but it is desirable that they be recognisably of the same shape. In the G language the shape is called the graph 'type' and provides the linking mechanism from one level in the graph hierarchy to another. Note that there is no restriction on the designer firing the same data operator more than once if he so desires.

The third divergence from software practice is that, as implied under (2) above, the inputs and outputs of a data operator are not to be regarded as values or references temporarily associated with it but are permanently connected. Of course, the lower level definition of the operator as a graph pair will use 'formal parameters' to express its structure, but the substitution of actual parameters in the form of the operator's genuine inputs and outputs is, like storage allocation, static. In software terms the closest analogy is 'call-by-name' in which each occurrence of a formal parameter in a procedure definition is replaced by the name of the actual parameter. The analogy is incomplete, of course, since in true call-by-name languages, such as Algol 60, the substitution must be made at run-time. Semantically, the inputs and outputs of an operator must be seen as physically identical to those of the lower-level graph.

4.1.6 The scope of the data

Virtually all programming languages allow a selection of different scope rules for variables. In block-structured languages the usual practice is to have local, static or global data. Local variables are dynamically allocated on the stack. Static and global variables have fixed locations but, while globals are available from anywhere in the program, statics can only be referenced from within the lexical scope of their declaration. Other languages, such as FORTRAN, distinguish between 'local' (in fact static) storage and 'common' areas used for communication between sub-programs. The requirements of formal analysis mean that in G only static data cells and busses are allowed. The analysis programs must be aware of every operator potentially writing to or reading from a given internal data cell in order to diagnose indeterminacy. The consequence of this is that every data cell or bus used at more than one graph level must be passed from level to level as an input and/or output parameter, using the procedure outlined at the end of the last section. If a cell or bus is not passed as a parameter it must be declared within the graph in which it is used.

4.2   THE REQUIREMENTS OF A GRAPH LANGUAGE

The following is a summary of the key properties which must be present
in a language intended to express the features of IDES graphs:

1) It must reflect the division between control and data while
providing a convenient cross-referencing mechanism.

2) The arbitrarily parallel structure of the control graph
must be represented.

3) The use of special control operators and complex subgraphs
must be catered for.

4) There must be a natural method of linking the graph levels
in a design.

In addition, the language should, as part of the IDES system, be reasonably easy to use and avoid assumptions about the user's intentions
which are extraneous to the formal model (such as having built-in
primitive data operators).

4.2.1   Overview and lexical conventions of G

G is a language for describing directed graphs according to the IDES
graph model. The compiler for the language is written in C [25] using
a YACC [29] generated parser and utilising the common IDES lexical
analyser. As such the language (intentionally) has many of the syntactic features of C.

A G program describes a single graph pair. It consists of a set of
'preprocessor specifications', followed by a 'preamble' giving the
name of the graph and its associated inputs and outputs and a 'body'
specifying the shape of the graph:

        preprocessor declarations

        example(input_parameter_list:output_parameter_list) {

            cell and bus declarations

            operator declarations

            control graph description

        }

Preprocessor declarations are simply a mechanism for giving symbolic names to numeric values which may be used in a description:

        #define SHIFT 16

This example defines the text string 'SHIFT' as having the equivalent numeric value '16'. Such defines are not processed by the G compiler but are stored within the generated data structure for later use by the lower level software (implementation and realisation). If it is required to use many 'defines' or to ensure that a particular symbol has the same value in a number of graph descriptions then the 'defines' may be collected together in a file and that file 'included' in with the current description:

        #include 'declarations_file'

where 'declarations_file' is any usual file-system pathname.

   The form of the preamble is deliberately the same as that of a data operator declaration and will be dealt with under that heading. The body of the graph is in three main parts, in the following strict order:

1) Declaration of data cells and data busses, with possible initialisation.

2) Declaration of data operators by type, with their connections to cells and busses.

3) Specification of the control graph, with cross-referencing to the data graph.

This ordering of parts prevents 'forward reference' problems and contributes to making the compiler single pass. It also tends to clarify the structure of the G program. In common with many programming languages, G has a fixed set of reserved keywords. In the ensuing text these will be underlined for clarity if they appear in an example. In practice, of course, they are not underlined and the user must refrain from trying to use them for the names of data cells, operators and so forth.

As can be seen from the example above the body of the graph appears between braces ('{' and '}') and parameters are surrounded by brackets ('(' and ')'). The G compiler accepts free-form input: newlines, spaces and tabs delimit a keyword or user-defined name but have no other significance. It is felt that program layout contributes greatly to comprehensibility but style is a matter of individual taste and should not be forced on the user. Statements in G, of which there are several kinds, must all be terminated by a semicolon (';'). Comments are surrounded by a two character escape sequence:

/* This would be a valid comment */

and may be used anywhere, except within a keyword or user-defined name:

/* this is a valid comment */ graph1/* so is this */
(in_params:out_params) /* and this */ {

Comments are totally ignored by the compiler and so this example is syntactically equivalent to:

graph1(in_params:out_params) {

User-defined names must consist of no more than 10 alphanumeric characters (letters, digits and '_'), commencing with a letter. Upper and lower case characters may be mixed indiscriminately and the cases are not mapped (i.e. the distinction is preserved). However, to allow the use of older types of computer terminal, keywords may be typed in either case, providing the cases are not mixed within a word.

Numbers in G are assumed to be decimal unsigned integers unless the first digit is a '0', in which case an octal interpretation is used (e.g. 0377 = 255). No negative or floating-point numbers are allowed.

4.3 THE DATA GRAPH

4.3.1 Cells and busses

The G compiler distinguishes between 'internal' and 'external' data cells and data busses. Externals are simply the inputs and outputs of the graph and are named in the preamble. In this context they stand for connections to the external environment and so they are represented uniformly as cells. This causes no loss of generality since, for the purposes of analysis, the distinction between an external cell and an external bus is significant not within the graph itself but at the higher level in which it is embedded. Internal cells and busses must be declared thus:

```
dcell    latch1,latch2,temp;
dbus     path,interrupt;
```

Note that bus declaration types must be used to declare objects which may be simultaneously read and written in order that this situation will not later be flagged as indeterminate. Multiple declaration statements like these may appear in any order in the first part of the graph body.

The initial values of data cells may be changed from the default value of 0:

        dcell   counter = 4, mask = 017,

These 'values' are not interpreted by the G compiler but are simply stored as numbers in the data structure. This is again due to the uninterpreted nature of the description. At the G level neither the eventual implementation of data cells nor the values they may contain have any effect on the analysis of the graph. The software at Level 2 may interpret the initial values in any way it likes, but there is no interpretation at the G level. It should be noted that the initialisation is static and refers to the value associated with a cell before it is first written to. Data busses, of course, only hold values while they are being written to and so cannot be initialised.

Data cells may also be given a 'width' (in bits). This, like initialisation, is done at declaration time:

        dcell   count<8> = 4;

As with initialisation this information is never used at level 1 and is simply stored by the compiler. If, for example, a 2-bit data cell were initialised to hold 23456:

        dcell   mistake<2> = 23456;

the impossibility of this situation would only be detected at implementation time. If no width is given for a cell or bus then the implementation software ensures that this gap is filled.

4.3.2   Data operators

The second part of the graph body in G serves two functions: providing the declaration of the data operators according to type and simultaneously describing the relatively simple topology of the data graph. For example, a sample data graph might be represented as:

> type add a1(in1,in2:temp1),a2(in3,temp1:temp2);
> type divide d1(temp1,temp2:out1,out2);

The operators a1 and a2 are declared to be of type 'add' and the operator d1 to be of type 'divide'. The bracketed list of arguments after each operator consists of inputs followed by outputs, separated by a colon. Each input and output must have been previously declared as a cell or bus, or be an external connection to the graph (i.e. be mentioned in the preamble as a parameter of the graph name). There is no fixed minimum or maximum number of inputs or outputs. The following operator declarations are all legal:

> x1(:out1,out2),x2(:),x3,
> x4(in1,in2,in3,in4,in5,in6.......:)

Strictly, of course, every operator should have at least one output, but this is checked by the Valid program at a later stage. As can be seen, the declaration of an operator has the same form as the graph preamble. This is because the operator type ('add' or 'divide' in the example) is actually the name of another graph in the hierarchy. The graph definition for 'add' might begin:

> add(arg1,arg2:result) {
>   etc.

The arguments to 'a1' and 'a2' must correspond both in number and order with the formal parameters in the definition of 'add'. Since graphs are produced one at a time the only checking which can be done by Valid is that 'a1' and 'a2' have consistent arguments. Whether they in fact correspond with the formal parameters must be checked in the context of the entire hierarchy (implementation feature).

There is no rule against a data operator having the same name as a type, but no implicit association is made if this is done:

```
type add divide(in1,in2:out1);
type divide add(in1,in2:out1,out2);
type xyz xyz(in1:out1,out2);              (a)
```

are all legal declarations. The situation in line (a) was found to occur quite often in worked examples, since in many cases there is only one operator of a given type. A shorthand form was introduced to make this more legible:

```
self abc(i1,i2:o1),def(:i4),ghi(o1,i1,i4:o2);
```

is equivalent to:

```
type abc abc(i1,i2:o1);
type def def(:i4);
type ghi ghi(o1,i1,i4:o2);
```

Since the rules of data graph topology require a strict alternation between operator and bus or cell the notation above is sufficient to completely describe it.

4.4   THE CONTROL GRAPH

4.4.1   Names

The description of the control graph is given in terms of the data operator, cell and bus names declared for the data graph. A control operator name is normally the same as that of the corresponding data node but without any associated arguments. However, there are three possible exceptions to this convention:

1) If a data node is referenced from two or more different places in the control graph it is necessary to distinguish the different 'instances' of its activation. This is done by modifying the operator name by the addition of an 'extension number'. For example:

add,add.1,add.017

are three different control operators firing the same data operator 'add'. The expression of the control graph structure may require a particular instance to be referred to more than once so it would not be possible to regard each occurrence of the basic name as a separate instance. The numbers are of no significance in themselves and may be anywhere in the range 1 to 255 (an extension of 0 is equivalent to no extension).

2) Syntax And operators cause no data graph activity and so are represented by a special symbol: '&'. If more than one Syntax And occurs in the control graph they may be distinguished by the use of extension numbers as for normal operators. Note, incidentally, that Syntax Ands, while never necessary, can significantly reduce the apparent complexity of a parallel structure.

3) The Blockhead and Blockend operators do not fire any data node and may be represented by '<' and '>' respectively. This also applies to Start and End nodes of complex subgraphs.

4.4.2   Structure

It is possible that the structure of the control graph could have been described by the same mechanism as used for the data graph, but two factors militated against such an approach. First, the control graph is homogeneous. It cannot be partitioned into two disjoint sets of nodes in the way that the data graph can, and so does not readily adapt to the form 'name(inputs:outputs)'. Second, the use of complex subgraphs meant that a syntax of this type would lead to tortuous and incomprehensible programs.

The solution eventually reached may be illuminated by considering the purpose of G as a means of describing parallel activity in contrast with a conventional language which is primarily serial. A language such as Algol 68 assumes that statements are executed consecutively unless a special syntax is used to show them in parallel. The G language inverts this attitude and considers everything to be in parallel unless a sequence is specified. A simple sequence is represented thus:

        a : b;

meaning 'there is an arc from a to b'. Sequences may be joined together, making 'chains':

        a : b : c : d;

with the obvious connotation of a path going through a, b, c and d. This method would be sufficient to completely describe any control graph structure, but for legibility a shorthand may be used, called a 'list':

        a : b,c,d;

is equivalent to:

        a : b; a : c; a : d;

Lists can also be used in chains. For example:

```
        a,b,c : d,e,f;
        a,b,c : & : d,e,f;
```

These chains are semantically equivalent, specifying control paths
from all nodes in the set 'a,b,c' to all nodes in the set 'd,e,f'.
(These forms are not however equivalent at lower levels in IDES since
the second form would lead to a different realisation.)

Chains may be of any length, and are terminated by a semicolon. A
control graph description consists of a set of chains in no particular
order. Topologically, a control graph with no subgraphs is a 'lat-
tice', since it imposes a 'partial ordering' on its constituent nodes,
is acyclic and contains two extremal nodes (the Blockhead and Blockend)

It was mentioned that the symbols for Blockhead and Blockend were
'<' and '>':

```
        < : a,b.2 : c;
        b.2,d : >;
```

An alternative notation is also accepted:

```
        : a,b.2 : c;
        b.2,d : ;
```

A null on the left or right of a colon is taken to mean the same as
'<' or '>' respectively. However, while

```
        a : b,>,c;
```

is legal,

```
        a : b,,c;
```

is not, and will be objected to by the compiler. In this book the symbols '<' and '>' will be used for clarity. Note that the Blockhead need not appear at the beginning nor the Blockend at the end of the control graph description, but neither may be omitted entirely.

4.4.3 Test operators

While normal control nodes have the names of operators in the data graph, all 'Test' control operators read data cells or busses directly, and consequently use their names instead. Extension numbers are employed for the same purpose as outlined above. In this section the various Test operators will be described in turn, using only simple subgraphs. Complex subgraphs are discussed in a later section. There are three types of Test operator:

1) The If:

if condition then xyz;

In this example 'condition' is a data cell or bus and 'xyz' a data operator. There is an optional 'else' part:

if condition then xyz else abc;

2) The While:

while condition do xyz;

The 'do' part may be omitted to give the effect of a WAIT operation:

while condition;

3) The Switch:

```
switch data_cell {
case SHIFT: shift;
case ADD,PLUS,SUM: add;
default: multiply;
};
```

The 'default' is optional. If it is not present and no 'case' is used the action is null. There may be no more than one 'default' and it can appear anywhere in the list of 'cases'.

With regard to the 'switch' operator the following points may be made:

i) Case values are uninterpreted strings. They are not associated with any data cells, but with the cases themselves. At lower levels in IDES (realisation) case values must be numerics in a range valid for the tested data cell. The usual way of managing this is to '#define' the value strings used at level 1.

ii) It is permissible to have multiple comma-separated values associated with any case. This should reduce the size of the G program by avoiding unnecessary duplication of sections of the control graph.

iii) The braces '{' and '}' are used, as with the graph body itself, to delimit the list of cases. They must still be followed by a semicolon if the switch is at the right-hand end of a chain. As will be explained shortly, braces are also used to surround a complex subgraph. It is important to note that the list of cases for a switch is not in itself a subgraph, but a set of subgraphs.

The test parts of the 'if' or 'while' operators may be negated:

```
if not condition then xyz else abc;
```

while not condition;

This is not possible for the 'switch', since its tested value is not interpreted as boolean. The simple subgraphs for any test operator can of course be other test operators:

```
while a do if b then c else d;
switch a {
        case AA: if b then c;
        case BB: while not d;
        default: switch e {
                case CC: f;
                case DD: g;
        };
};
```

In this context it should be noted that the 'dangling else' problem is solved in the usual way:

```
if a then if b then c else d;
```

The 'else' operator 'd' is associated with the nearest surrounding 'if' i.e. 'b'.

The syntax of these operators is reasonably self-explanatory. However, if a test operator is referenced more than once in a control graph description, it is pointless to require a repetition of its complete specification. The rule, therefore, is that a complete definition of the structure of the operator and its subgraphs may appear only once, and other references are by means of the name alone:

```
a : if b then c;
b : d : e : >;
```

In fact it is not necessary to give the full form before using the

74

name. The above example may equally well be written:

```
b : d : e : >;
a : if b then c;
```

An alternative, and briefer, form would be:

```
a : if b then c : d :e : >;
```

where the two chains are combined. Note that the path goes from b to
d, not from c to d. The condition part of a Test operator acts as its
name in every context, including chains and lists.

4.4.4   Complex subgraphs

Complex subgraphs are a phenomenon of the control graph topology. They
have no effect on the data graph and cause no stacking of the name environment. Thus a name in a subgraph refers to the same instance as
the same name outside it, although a G program containing both is in
error. Subgraphs are enclosed in braces:

```
while a do {
        < : b,c : d : e,f;          (a)
        e : g,h : >;                (b)
        f : >;                      (c)
   };
```

Within the braces the symbols '<' and '>' (lines (a), (b) and (c))
refer not to the Blockhead and Blockend of the total graph but to the
Start and End nodes of the subgraph. Once again, nulls can be used in
their place, with the same restrictions.

Complex subgraphs can appear anywhere that simple subgraphs can, and
may be nested to any depth:

```
< : a, if b then {
        < : c,d :>;
} else while e do {
        < : f, switch g {
            case AA: {
                    < : h,i,j : >;
            };
            case BB:

            etc.
```

4.5   ANALYSIS PROGRAMS

Once a graph data structure has been produced by the G compiler (or by
the graphics system) it must be rigorously checked for two main
classes of error:

  1) Topological errors which imply that the data structure does
  not   describe a structurally correct graph. For example, the
  control graph might contain cycles, some control operator
  might not be on a path from the BH, and so on.

  2) Determinacy errors which mean that the operation of the
  graph pair cannot be guaranteed always to give the same effect
  i.e. it might exhibit time dependent behaviour.

These correctness properties are verified by two programs, called
respectively 'valid' and 'determ'. The reasons for having two programs rather than one are that a) there is a clear separation of function between the two programs, which check for different types of error in different ways and b) the checking of determinacy depends on
the validity of the data structure i.e. 'determ' must refuse to try
and analyse a data structure which has not first been passed by
'valid'.   To this end the data structure as stored in a disk file has
a status word at the beginning, containing bits set by the various

programs through which it passes. In this way the history of the data
structure can to some extent be reconstructed.

4.5.1   Valid

The 'valid' program checks for some 32 distinct error conditions, of
which 27 are fatal and 5 are warnings. For many of these it is help-
ful to convert the linked-list form of the data structure to an in-
cidence matrix representation.   In this form the presence of a 1 in
position (i,j) means there is an arc from node i to node j. The transitive closure of the matrix representing the CG is then constructed
using Warshall's Algorithm [30]. A 1 in position (i,j) now means that
there is a 'path' from i to j. Clearly, if the diagonal of the transitive closure (positions (i,i) for all i) contains any 1's, the CG
has cycles in it, since some nodes must have paths to themselves.
This is the first thing checked by 'valid'. If the graph fails this
test it is immediately rejected, since many of the remaining structural properties of the CG then become very difficult to verify.

Assuming that the CG has passed this test, the most difficult property still to be checked is that it consists of a correctly structured set of nested subgraphs. It may be thought that this problem is
suitable for recursive solution, since the syntax of nested subgraphs
can be recursively described (this has no bearing at all on whether or
not graphs can describe recursive functions). However, it should be
realised that, since the structure itself is being examined to see if
it is recursive, this is perhaps not the best approach. A suitable
algorithm has been devised and implemented.

The remaining properties examined by 'valid' include ensuring that
every cell and bus is used (read or written by a data operator or
tested from the CG), that all 'case' values for a given Switch are
distinct, that a Switch has only one 'default' branch, that an If has
exactly one 'then' and at most one 'else' and so on. Many of these
error conditions cannot happen if the compiler is working properly,

since they cannot be expressed in legal G, but a graphics input system may not be able to check these things for itself. In any case, if a data structure is declared to be correct it should be so.

There is, inevitably, a qualification. Since graphs are tested in isolation from each other it is possible to have two kinds of un-discovered error. There may be a mismatch between the numbers of inputs and/or outputs declared in the graph header and the number used when the graph name appears as a type. Furthermore, it is possible to define mutually recursive graphs (A uses B, which uses A) and this is meaningless. Both these properties could be checked but this would best be done by a total design checker which has has yet to be written.

4.5.2 Determ

The determinacy of a graph pair is often its most important feature, since without it the graph cannot be used reliably. In this context 'determinacy' means the property that, although nodes are being initiated asynchronously and in parallel, the result of any activation of the graph ('result' being interpreted as the total configuration of values in all the data cells after the graph has terminated) depends solely on the initial configuration of data and the transformations performed by the data operators. In practical terms, this is reduced to the two requirements:

1) That no data cell may be simultaneously written to by one data operator and read by another or tested by a control operator.

2) That no data cell may be written to simultaneously by two data operators.

The two corresponding error conditions are called respectively read/write and write/write indeterminacy. During the development of the IDES Level 1 system it was realised that some configurations e.g multiple processor computers, were intrinsically indeterminate by these criteria. This is because they do not really have a single controller, although it is still desired to represent them with a single CG at some level. Such systems must synchronise through data operations. For example, a CPU communicating with some memory through a bus controls its own actions internally by setting or examining status information which is in some sense external to it (i.e. not exclusively internal) and is shared with the memory, which is also acting independently. Now it is desired to be able to show such a system as a DG, with the CPU and memory as data operators and the status information as data cells to which they write and from which they read. (Note, incidentally, that the memory is not a simple data cell at this level of detail.) However, for the scheme to represent a real situation it is essential for the CPU and memory to be able to examine or set the status cells whenever they wish, which includes simultaneously. This immediately gives both read/write and write/write conflicts. It is important to note that this example is not entirely artificial. Genuine hardware systems are in this sense indeterminate, but they manage to get over the problem most of the time by means of rigorous timing constraints.

The formal model of asynchronous operation is essentially inadequate in the above situation, possibly because the dichotomy between control and data is too strict to represent the reality of physical devices. Nevertheless, it was felt it to be a useful model for describing the structure of algorithms, so it was desirable to retain it. This was the motivation for the introduction of data busses, which had been absent in all previous models. Thus, if the phrase 'no data cell may' is replaced by 'every data cell must' in the first of the above definitions of indeterminacy we obtain the requirement for the use of a data bus to be considered correct. That is to say, a data bus must be read from and written to simultaneously. Note that the reading can take the form of testing from the CG. It is also permissible for two or more data operators to simultaneously read from a data bus. The use of the data bus has the effect of reducing the number of spurious faults thrown up by determinacy checking, this being a failing of the original LOGOS system.

The program 'determ' which checks these various conditions, again uses a matrix representation of the graph data structure. In this case, the transitive closure matrix of the CG is used to determine which pairs of data operators can be active in parallel. These are precisely the pairs of operators whose corresponding CG nodes have a 0 in the appropriate position in the transitive closure matrix i.e. if position (i,j) is empty, then DG nodes i and j may be active in parallel (since there is no path between their control operators, and hence no sequence is specified). The input and output data cells are then examined to see if there is overlap.

It transpires that if the CG was allowed to contain cycles (aside from the limited form of the While) it would not be sufficient to check the static topology to catch determinacy errors. This is because arbitrary cycles can only be represented if there is another kind of control node (called an 'or') whose function is to merge alternative control paths. This changes the input firing rule for that node, since it must fire once for each one input to its control cell (otherwise firings would get lost), and it becomes possible to construct graphs in which a single control one at one point is multiplied into a sequence of ones at a later point. This cannot happen with the revised model since, although a CG operator may emit more ones than it absorbs, these are all on distinct arcs. It is thus impossible to generate multiple firings of a later CG operator from a single initial one. This was a major problem for the workers at Case Western Reserve University, since they had to take the CG through every reasonable dynamic state in order to verify that it was determinate. This is a combinatorially exploding technique (in both time and space), to such an extent that the analysis of a CG containing only 9 nodes (including BH and BE) was declared to be unmanageable on a single-user PDP 11/45. This by current methods is not the case and CG's with many more nodes

(50-100) may be handled in seconds.

In the implementation of the analysis programs there is the further problem that, as has been shown earlier, there is a) no explicit connection between the End of a subgraph and its controlling If, While or Switch (this is to avoid what might look like cycles in the CG) and b) the alternative branches of an 'if' or 'switch' appear to be active in parallel. Determ has to show some intelligence in dealing with subgraphs, since the simple matrix calculations would in general show horrendous determinacy errors. Instead of including a lot of special case code, the approach is to change the structure of the CG in its matrix representation so that the algorithm which actually checks determinacy thinks that the subgraphs are 'in line' with the main part of the CG. Of course, it is purely a temporary and internal measure, and never appears in the graph data structure as seen by other programs.

4.5.3 Maxpar

It is at this point that the previously mentioned (chapters 2 and 3) manipulation to establish the maximally parallel version of the control graph is undertaken. Since a program exists to perform this function on the graph, it is actually unnecessary for the designer to consider whether or not any operations can be executed in parallel. He may merely list all the operations which have to be performed, as if they must be strictly sequential, and the facility will automatically provide the parallelism for him. It is a useful tool for investigating designs. An algorithm may require several instances of a similar operation, e.g. add. The designer may initially declare all the add operations as different instances of type add. If subsequent processing reveals that two instances of the add operation can never be active in parallel, then the designer may redesign his algorithm to utilise a single add operator for both instances with no loss of performance.

The basic algorithm for Maxpar is due to Bain [18] derived from a technique mentioned by Coffman and Denning [19]. The outline of the method of generating a maximally parallel control graph is as follows.

Determinacy is first established as this is a prerequisite for developing maximally parallel graphs. As described previously, determinacy is established by preparing the connectivity matrix M of the graph. M[i,j] is set to 1 if node i is connected to node j, 0 otherwise. The transitive closure matrix T is then generated using Warshall's [30] algorithm. An examination of T for all entries T[i,j] = 0 will yield all pairs of operators i and j which could be active in parallel as there is no path between i and j. Each pair is inspected for possible memory conflicts, and if none are found the graph is determinate. Having established this, the only conflicts which could possibly occur are between nodes on the same path. Two operators X and Y interfere with each other if there is a path from X to Y and the domains or ranges of X and Y overlap to any extent. The set of all interfering pairs is I. Having deleted all arcs from the control graph, a new control graph is constructed. There is a path from the blockhead (see Section 4.5) to any X such that there is no Y where (Y,X) is a member of I. An arc is inserted from X to Y for all pairs of operators X,Y such that (X,Y) is a member of I. Finally, all operators X such that there is no Y where (X,Y) is a member of I have arcs drawn from them to the blockend.

The resulting control graph is maximally parallel.

CHAPTER 5

Design Implementation

5.1   THE HARDWARE DESCRIPTION LANGUAGE HDL

The hardware description language (HDL) is concerned with the physical form of digital systems. Representation of a system is made firstly by declaring those objects comprising the system, secondly by defining the interconnection of those objects in terms of possible data paths and thirdly by specifying when those data paths are opened for data transfer. The activation of transfers is then specified in terms of control sequencing. The major part of the design effort thus becomes transferring the block diagram of the system into HDL and then adding the control information. As such the language can be considered as a register transfer language and a design as being a register transfer machine. It is this design effort which is aided by the implementation level of the IDES software suite. The implementation software takes a G description of a design and interactively implements it under the designer's guidance. It produces an HDL description of the design as the output from this process. Naturally, the implementation program produces a syntactically and semantically correct HDL description. Since this description is in the form of a text file, and HDL is basically a textual description, then the designer can design in HDL, or take an implemented G description and edit it. Both situations could result in a description containing erroneous syntax or semantics, and would cause the realisation software to fail. To enable designers to understand the output from the implementation program, to design directly in HDL, or to modify implemented designs, HDL is introduced in detail in the following sections.

5.1.1   The specification of HDL

The objects between which transfers are made are not simply considered as being registers and are completely general. The language has no inbuilt types or primitives (e.g. register, memory etc.) but being a design language will accept any specification the user gives and search for something which suits that application. The blocks in the designer's block diagram are purely conceptual and only at a later realisation phase need they be associated will real components (chips or circuits). The objects used within a design may be chips (integrated circuits) or previously specified designs. In fact the designer need not know how an object will be realised, thus giving a truly hierarchical design language.

Transfers are made between conceptual 'ports' on an object. A port is defined as being a collection of signals of similar or related function and there are mechanisms in the language for referring to a port either by a user defined name or by a more rigid syntactic representation of function. The specification of a transfer may take a number of forms which allow the wide range of information transfers that exist in real designs. A transfer, or group of transfers, may be given a name which can be used in the control specification to indicate when the transfer(s) should be activated.

The descriptive mechanism used for control flow is very similar to that used in the IDES Level 1 language G (chapter 4) and allows for arbitrary parallelism in the design, structuring of the control flow based upon a data dependent branch mechanism and other high-level constructs such as switching of control paths based upon generated data values.

5.1.2 Overview and lexical conventions of HDL

HDL is a language for describing digital circuits in terms of their separate data and control flow. The compiler for the language is written in C using a YACC generated parser and utilising the common IDES lexical analyser. As such the compiler supports the same lexical conventions as all other IDES text parsing programs.

Names must commence with a letter and must consist of no more than 10 alphanumeric characters. The alphanumeric set consists of letters, digits and certain other special symbols (e.g. '_','#','$'). Upper and lower case characters may be mixed indiscriminately and the cases are not mapped (i.e. the distinction is preserved).

As in G, numbers are assumed to be decimal unsigned integers, unless the first digit is a zero in which case an octal interpretation is used (e.g. 0377 = 255). No negative or floating point numbers are allowed.

Comments are specified by surrounding them with the usual two character escape sequence:

    /* This would be a valid comment */

and may be used anywhere except within a keyword or user defined name. Comments are stripped out by the lexical analyser and so are totally ignored by the compiler. Line and character counting is maintained correctly and generated error messages reflect this.

A further feature supported by the lexical analyser is that of preprocessor declarations in exactly the same way as in a G description (chapter 4). In essence this is a simple mechanism for giving symbolic names to numeric values which may be used in the description. Within the HDL compiler all preprocessor declarations must precede the body of the design.

If it is required to use many such definitions, or to ensure that a symbol has the same value in a number of design descriptions then the defines may be collected together in a file and that file included in the current design:

        #include "declarations_file"

where 'declarations_file' is any usual filesystem name.

5.1.3   The structure of descriptions

An HDL program describes a single digital design. It consists of a set of pre-processor specifications, followed by a preamble giving the name of the design and its associated input and output ports, and a body specifying the internal detail of the design.

        preprocessor declarations

        design name (input_port_list : output_port_list)

        {

                component declarations

                transfer declarations

                control flow description

        }

The form of the preamble is deliberately the same as that used in all other language descriptions within IDES. Starting with the name of the design we have a comma separated list specifying the names of the input ports and the output ports for that design.

```
newdesign1(inport1,inport2:outport1,outport2)
{

        design description

}
```

There are no restrictions on the number of I/O ports which may be given, though to be strictly correct every design should have at least one output. Port names in the preamble may be optionally followed by a bit-width. If this is omitted, the port is assumed to be one bit wide. As can be seen from the example above, the port list is surrounded by brackets ('(',')') and the body of the graph appears between braces ('{','}').

The HDL compiler accepts free form input. Newlines, spaces and tabs delimit a keyword or user defined name but have no other significance and are, in fact, stripped out by the lexical analyser. Each statement must be terminated by a semi-colon (';').

5.1.4   Component declarations

This, the first portion of the body, is concerned with declaring those components which will be referenced in the transfers section. Declarations are made in terms of conceptual blocks (e.g. register, memory, counter etc.). These do not correspond to any inbuilt type names and, for any boxtype the designer specifies, the software simply looks for a circuit or chip of that name. The declaration statement allows not only for the declaration of a boxtype but for the declaration of a number of attributes associated with the boxes of that type. Following the boxtype is a list of the required instances of that type, each of which may have associated dimensions in words ('[',']') and/or bits ('<','>'). Bit widths may be omitted, a default value of 1 being assumed.

```
counter(up,down)  a<4>,b<8>;
memory(rom)       c[16]<8>;
```

This example declares two up/down counters 'a' and 'b' of differing widths and a read-only memory 'c'. The attribute list is of equal importance to the object type declaration since each attribute is associated with each box instance given. The compiler internally makes no distinction between an object type and its attributes when it comes to selecting components at realisation time. The first declaration could equally well have been made as:

    up(counter,down) a<4>,b<8>;

Compilation error messages and diagnostics often refer to a particular boxtype, not simply to the instance name of a box. In this case, messages would refer to an 'up'. Thus it is good policy to specify the main feature of an object as being its type. For every declaration given the compiler will search for the object directly (by name):

    thiscounter   x<6>;

The realisation process in the above case would look for a design or chip which had the name 'thiscounter' and if found would load all the necessary information about that component. Realisation therefore operates in two modes.   In one mode, when the boxtype is uniquely specified, information is loaded at declaration time so that meaningful error messages may be generated as each line of input is processed. If the declaration is only a partial specification, allowing some selection of components, then only when the complete description has been processed and all information accumulated regarding the function of the box will a selection be made. Though component selection may be carried out at a number of points in the realisation process, it is done in exactly the same way in each case (common routine) and operates on the internal data structure. Basic to chip selection is a knowledge of how to expand certain objects bit-wise (the object declared has to be formed from multiple chips of lesser bit-width). When required, the selection software will automatically carry out expansion upon the selected component to form a circuit of suitable width. The specification of expansion algorithms is catered for in the integrated circuit description language (ICDL) and is described in chapter 6. This expansion facility has not yet been built into the circuit description language (CDL) and so only integrated circuits may be automatically expanded. This expansion mechanism is only for the bit-wise replication of components and there is no capability for functional expansion as yet.

Following any instance declaration there may be an initialisation statement.

        register a<4>=7;

This initialisation allows for an object to be loaded with a particular value on 'power-up'. This initialisation is once-only and is not repeated upon successive activations of the control circuitry.

Having said that there are no inbuilt types, we now make an exception. It may be desired to include a previously designed component in the current design in a one-off fashion. The object declaration for this` is unnecessarily long-winded and an abbreviated form has been built into the language utilising the keyword 'self':

        self   mul16,convert;

This declares the use of two circuits (mul16 and convert) whose instance names are the same as their boxtypes. Busses, which to all intents and purposes are considered by the designer as distinct objects, do not exist as such. To inform the compiler of this situation an object name can be given the boxtype 'bus':

        bus   x<6>;

This statement declares a databus 'x' which is 6 bits wide.

5.1.5   Transfer declarations

Transfer declarations specify paths along which data may flow between components in the design. In general, a transfer gives a directed connection between two objects: the source object and the sink object.

5.1.5.1 Object specification

An object is defined as being a bit or number of bits on a specific port on a named component (instance) :

instance-spec '.' port-spec '<' bit-spec '>'

Each part of this specification will be treated separately.

An instance specification is a name which has been given in a previous component declaration. If the instance portion of an object specification is omitted then the remaining information is assumed to apply to the current design (i.e. the port name must be one of the port names specified in the design preamble).

Port specifications are made in one of two forms, either directly as a port name or as a port identifier. There should be no mixing of these two forms. All references to ports on an instance of a component should use the same port specification syntax. Port names are simply those names which are mentioned in the preamble to a description and may be used freely in higher level descriptions. Port identifiers are built up by using one of 5 generic port types:

I	Input
O	Output
A	Address
F	Function
B	Bus

in conjunction with a numeric value in square brackets ('[',']') :

     I[3]   Input port three

     A[1]   Address port one

If a port specification is omitted from the object specification then
the compiler assumes that there is only one suitable port. For example, if the object specification is being used as the source in a
transfer then the compiler will assume that there is only one output
port. If this assumption proves to be invalid, the compiler will generate error messages.

Bit specifications are given in angle brackets ('<','>') and define
those bit(s) which are to be considered as part of the transfer. Any
number of bits (up to the width of the port) may be given provided
that they are given in ascending order. This restriction has been rigidly enforced since it gives a 'least likely error' situation with
respect to bit transpositions. The generalised bit specification is a
comma separated list of bit numbers, individual numbers being in the
range from zero to the port width minus one. In place of any single
bit number a bit range may be given as an abbreviated form for listing
many sequential bits. Some valid bit specifications (and their expanded equivalent) might be:

     <0>   <0>

     <0,2-4>   <0,2,3,4>

     <1,3-5,6,8-9> <1,3,4,5,6,8,9>

     <2-6>   <2,3,4,5,6>

Similarly, in place of a bit number certain keywords have been provided to cope with situations where the designer does not know the bit
range of a port:

     LSB   Least significant bit

     MSB   Most significant bit

The use of these keywords must still conform with the rule of ascendance:

        `<0,LSB,4-5>`   Invalid specification
        `<LSB,4-5,MSB>` Valid specification (iff MSB > 5)

A simple extension (not implemented as yet) is the use of arithmetic expressions based upon simple numbers and keywords which could be used to form a bit-specification:

        `<LSB+1,MSB/2>`

This form of specification is useful when the number of bits to be transferred is dependent upon the width of the port and thus on the components eventually selected.

The use of abbreviated forms keywords and arithmetic expressions is restricted to situations where the compiler knows, or can compute, absolute values (i.e. the component has been successfully selected from information given in the instance declarations). If a bit specification is completely omitted, then full port width is assumed.

5.1.5.2 Transfer specification

There are four basic transfer types; simple transfers, loads, assertions and tests. All transfers are specified in terms of what the designer wants to do, not how he wishes to do it. For example, in order that a transfer may be made between specified objects then, depending upon the objects concerned, it may be necessary to enable certain other ports or facilities on the objects themselves. This is not taken care of by the designer, but automatically by the realisation software. Similarly the discrete connections and (possibly) gating required in order to connect the individual bits in a transfer are generated automatically. These operations must be taken care of in this manner, since it is only with a knowledge of the chips and cir-

cuits that are used in the final realisation that appropriate gating
and buffering can be known.

A 'simple transfer' specifies the bit-wise connection of one object
to another:

        a.parout<0-3> -> b.address<0-3>;

In this example 4 bits on the parout port of object a are transferred
to the address port on object b. In this case the port names used
give a fair idea of the type of ports that are actually involved.
Further, the bits in the transfer are the same in both cases and are
the low-order 4 bits on the port. More generally, the bits in
transfers will not be the same:

        a.parout<0,1,2,3> -> b.address<0,4-6>;

If no bit specification is given in either the source or sink of a
transfer then the connection applies across the full width of the
port. Therefore if the width of the parout and address ports was 4
bits the the example above could be given as:

        a.parout -> b.address;

Similarly if there was only one port on each of these objects which
could conceivably be used, then the port specification may be omitted
and we have the simple transfer:

        a -> b;

Utilising all the defaults in conjunction is specifically forbidden,
for, though the statement:

        . -> .

by the previously described rules would mean 'connect the one input
port on this design to the one output port on this design over their
full bit width', the construction of the parser is such that the
statement would cause internal ambiguities. There must be either an
instance or a port specification in every object specification.

In certain applications it is desired to transfer a constant value
to a port (e.g. initialising a counter). This is catered for in the
HDL by the load transfer type. Using this facility a numeric value
may be loaded into a port or specific bits on a port. The numeric
value itself may be presented in a number of forms. As a decimal
number:

        12 -> a.parin<0-3>;

or in octal form:

        014 -> a.parin<0-3>;

or as a binary list:

        1,1,0,0 -> a.parin<0-3>;

These three examples all represent the same transfer, though each have
specific contexts in which they may best be used. Decimal numbers are
best used in a context where the number itself has meaning for the
designer, whereas octal numbers are preferable when trying to load
specific bits on a port. The binary list facility is provided as a
second form of octal loading so that only certain bits in a port may
be asserted or deasserted. For example:

        1,0,0,1 -> x<2,4,6,7>;

whilst asserting bits 2 and 7 and deasserting bits 4 and 6 will not
change any other bits in the sink port. In contrast, loading a

decimal/octal number will assert all those bits required to represent that number and will deassert all other bits. The assertion or deassertion required in loading a number will affect only those bits specified in the sink of the transfer:

        13 -> x.data<0-6>;

will leave the bits above bit 6 untouched. This facility is completely general, in that it is possible to load a number into certain restricted bits in a port:

        13 -> x.data<0,3,6,9,12>;

This statement would give rise to the assertion of bits 0,6,9 and the deassertion of bits 3 and 12, all other bits remaining as they were prior to the enabling of the transfer. (Note that the lowest bit (bit 0) is treated as having lowest numeric significance).

An assertion transfer type does not call for the transfer of data between objects, but is a manipulative operation upon an object. For example, a particular component may support an 'increment' function. This function can be activated by name through the use of an assertion:

        a.inc;

The increment function, 'inc', as specified in the description of 'a', which may be a sub-design (circuit) or an integrated circuit (chip) will be asserted each time this transfer is enabled. Although in many cases it may be correct (valid) to assert a particular bit on a port (e.g. the add function pin within the function port on an alu), the designer of a lower level component is assumed to have given names to all acceptable functions. So whilst the statement:

        x.F[1]<2>;

would, by the syntax rules of the language, be correct, it has been specifically prohibited in favour of named assertions of the form:

        x.add

where, internal to the description of component 'x', the function named 'add' is given the correct pin association. This restriction is not inherent in the compiler and could be removed at a future date if it was considered too restrictive.

The final transfer type is the test transfer. Tests are used to provide a data-dependent branch and loop facility in the control flow and for collecting together signals so that the end result may be used at a later time. A test is given in the form of a boolean expression relating bits within ports on a variety of objects. All the standard IDES boolean operators are supported and the standard IDES operator symbols are used:

        &   And
        ¦   Or
        !   Negate
        ^   Xor
        =   Equivalence

Operands in a boolean expression take the form of an object specification:

        a.out<3>&b.out<2>;

If the bit specification within an object specification contains more than one bit then it is assumed to be the or-ing of all the specified bits:

        a.out<3>&b.out<2,3>;

would be evaluated as:

a.out<3>&(b.out<2>|b.out<3>);

There are two forms of tests. Tests which result in a simple boolean
value (bit tests) and those which result in a number of bits (word
tests). The test expressions in both cases take the same form, though
in the bit test resulting bits are or-ed to form a single boolean signal.

5.1.5.3 Transfer timing

HDL allows the complete specification of a design without the engineer having to give consideration to details such as operation timing. The specification of control and its successive realisation ensures that an operation will be complete before another dependent
operation is initiated. However, a designer may wish to constrain an
operation (transfer) to take place within a certain timespan. This
puts limits on the speed of components it is possible to use, and effectively narrows the selection at realisation time. (Component timing information may still be entered as an attribute at declaration
time).

A timing constraint may be placed on any non-test type transfer by
entering a bracketed value of nano-seconds before the end of the
statement:

x -> y.in<0,2,5> (100);

Initially this might appear meaningless, since normally data transfers
are considered to take no time at all. It is to be remembered that a
transfer given at this level is eventually expanded, where necessary,
to encompass the enabling of the source of the transfer, the switching
logic required to route or buffer the data, the enabling of the sink
and finally a period of time required for that data to be latched.

5.1.5.4 Transfer modes

Any transfer which involves the explicit transfer of data (i.e. contains the transfer symbol '->') may be given an optional transfer mode. The transfer mode specifies the type of transfer which the designer wishes to use. For example, the designer might want a transfer to use tri-state gating. Transfer modes are specified using a single letter inserted into the transfer symbol:

    -T>   Tri-state
    -O>   Open-collector
    -M>   Multiplexed

The end result of such a statement is that all gating to the sink would be carried out normally, only the final gate being of the particular type specified and enabled appropriately by a control signal. The statement of transfer mode is in fact a forcing statement and need never be made, for if, during realisation, it is detected that a transfer is being made to a databus type port then the software will automatically or interactively select appropriate logic gating. If the designer specifies a transfer mode to a component then all other transfers to the same component must be similarly and consistently specified.

5.1.5.5 Transfer names

Any transfer declaration may be preceded by an optional transfer name.

        tran1 == transfer ;

It is this transfer name which is referred to in the control flow to denote when the transfer should be activated. If the transfer is not given a name then it is assumed to be always enabled (i.e. a direct connection).

Under certain conditions it is desirable to use the same name for a
number of different transfers so that they may be all activated by a
single control graph signal. This is done by specifying the transfers
as a comma separated list:

            tran1 == transfer , transfer , ... ;

If this form is not used (i.e. the same name is used twice) then multiple declaration errors will result.

When a name has to be associated with a test type transfer, a
slightly different assignment syntax must be used. The difference in
syntax informs the compiler as to whether the test expression to follow should be interpreted as a bit or a word test:

            test1 =b= ....
            test2 =w= ....

The names assigned to test type transfers are used in the control flow
as arguments to the test operators (described later).

5.1.6   Control specification

The specification of control, within the language, states when the
previously declared transfers are to be activated. This activation
information is given by relating the 'firing' of individual transfers
to each other in the form of control sequencing and is oriented towards concurrent operation. The control flow specification takes the
form of a directed graph with two extremal nodes i.e a unique start
and a unique end. The graph itself must be acyclic and the flow of
control such that all activations are on a path linking the start to
the end. These paths are specified in the form of sequencing statements. Unlike most other descriptive languages there is no implied
sequencing taken from the order in which statements are presented, the
sequencing of operations is explicit. All transfers are assumed to be

in parallel unless a sequence is specified.

5.1.6.1 Chains

Statements within the language simply state the transfer name(s) as given in the transfer declarations and specify which transfer(s) they must precede:

        tran1 : tran2;

This example states that 'tran1' must be activated and the transfer operation complete before 'tran2' is activated. The colon ':' is used as a sequence separator and, as with all other statement types in the language the semi-colon ';' is a statement terminator.

This syntax may be extended to express the sequencing of a number of transfers and this is termed a 'chain':

        tran1 : tran2 : tran3 ......;

Hence giving a control path from 'tran1' through 'tran2' etc.

5.1.6.2 Lists

Highly parallel structures often require that a single operation be followed (or preceded) by a number of other operations. This could be specified by a number of simple chains:

        a : b;
        a : c;
        a : d;

This construct appears so frequently that an alternative syntax termed a 'list' is allowed:

```
a : b , c , d;
```

A comma separated list of successors (or predecessors) may be used anywhere that a single transfer name would be valid. Use of this construct gives implied parallelism to the transfers b, c, d, but this would be overridden by any sequencing between members of the set, thus a list does not explicitly specify parallelism and is merely a syntactic convenience.

Lists may be used anywhere in a chain but it should be noted that the list separator ',' is more binding than the chain separator ':'. In the example:

```
a , b : c , d;
```

both the transfers a and b must be complete before either c or d may be activated i.e. there is a control flow connection from a to both c and d and similarly connections from b to both c and d.

5.1.6.3 Syntax operators

As there is no implicit start to the control specification, special operators are required to signify explicitly the start and end of the graph. These are introduced as:

```
start - <
end   - >
```

and may be used in place of a transfer name at any point:

```
< : a : b : >;
```

In this case giving a very simple graph where there is a simple serial chain from the start through a and b to the end. Since the start and end form the two extremal nodes in the graph, the start symbol cannot be used validly on the right hand side of a chain, nor the end symbol on the left. Put more simply, no transfers may be activated prior to the start nor after the end.

Quite complex interconnections may be very simply represented using lists in chains:

        a , b , c : d , e , f;

giving a schema in which all the nodes in the set a, b, c have connections to the nodes in the set d, e, f (9 links in all). There is, however, a more efficient way of specifying this form of linkage using a 'syntax-and' facility:

        a , b , c : & : d , e , f;

The operator '&' simply connects streams of control flow together (an anding operation). As such it forms a no-op in the control flow i.e. it is not associated with a transfer and is used in this example to reduce the number of inter-node links (down to 6). When the circuit is realised, the use of a syntax-and would result in reduced complexity in the control hardware.

5.1.6.4 Multiple activations

If a transfer is activated from more than one place in the control flow, it is necessary to distinguish the different instances of its activation. This is done by modifying the transfer name with the addition of an instance number:

        xx.1 : a.27 : xx.2

Omitting these extensions would have led to a cycle in the flow. Instance numbers have no significance in themselves and must be in the range 1-255. An extension of 0 is equivalent to no extension.

5.1.6.5 Conditional branching

In any realistic design, it is required to modify the action of the controller depending upon data input to, or generated by, the data flow. This takes the form of data-dependent branch and loop facilities based on the normal structured program constructs (if,while,switch) and utilises test type transfers previously described.

Straightforward branching is carried out using the 'if' operator:

    if (test-name) then transfer-name;

The transfer, 'transfer-name' is activated if the result of the test type transfer 'test-name' gives a truth value. An optional alternate action may be activated upon the failure of the test:

    if (test-name) then tran1 else tran2;

The 'else' part may be specified only if there is a 'then' part. To achieve activation of a transfer upon the failure (false return) of a test, the test itself may be negated:

    if (! test-name) then tran2 else tran1;

This effectively inverts the 'then' and 'else' parts of the previous example.

A similar construct is used to allow controlled looping in the flow. This looping does not form cycles in the graph since no explicit connections are made from the repetitively activated transfer to other transfers in the body of the description. The 'while' operator, as with the 'if', acts upon the result of a named test-type transfer:

    while (test-name) do transfer-name;

The test is evaluated and, if its result is true, then the specified transfer is activated. This process is repeated until the test returns false. As before, the test part may be inverted (negated) :

```
while ( ! test-name) do transfer-name;
```

The 'do' part of a 'while' is optional and may be omitted to give the effect of waiting for an event:

```
while ( test-name );
while ( ! test-name );
```

Negations used in tests are realised discretely for every activation. If the test is always used in an negated mode then it is more efficient to put the negation into the declaration of the test itself and test for a truth value.

The test operators described so far have utilised only binary (true/false) tests. The 'switch' operator utilises word tests to give a multiple branching action. This means that, depending upon the actual numeric value returned from a test, one of a number of possible actions may be selected:

```
switch ( test-name ) {
case    0 : tran0;
        .
case   27 : tran27;
        .
        .
case  224 : tran224;
};
```

It should be noted that the switch portion is surrounded by { and } and that, as it forms a statement in the language, it must be terminated (if no further connectivity is being specified) by a semi-colon. The arguments to the cases are numeric. This gives little significant information about an operation, and it is usual to use the preprocessor definitions to give symbolic names to these numbers. In order that all possible numeric outcomes of the test need not be specified, a 'default' action is provided and this will be enacted if no 'case' value is matched:

```
switch ( opcode-test ) {
case SHIFT : doshift;
case ADD   : doadd;
       .

       .

default    : trap;
};
```

A further extension allows multiple case values to be associated with a single action:

```
switch (data-test) {
case GOOD,MODERATE,POSITIVE : pass;
case BAD,INDIFFERENT,NEGATIVE : fail;
default: blow-up;
};
```

This mechanism allows a great reduction in the size of an HDL specification. Otherwise, switching would have to be done in the form of multiple nested 'if-then-else' tests, successively testing the bits in a controlling data-word.

In all the tests, flow of control continues directly from the test node itself and not from the activated transfers. The transfers activated are considered as being pendent upon the test operator, hanging on a branch which is not a normal control flow path. These transfers are only on a path from the start to the end if their associated test is. Connections must not be made directly between the main control flow and a pendent operation. In the case of the 'if' operator:

        a : if (test1) then b else c : d : e;

after having carried out the test and activating b or c depending upon its result, transfer d would be activated. This transfer follows on from the test and not from transfer c as it might at first appear. A separate and distinctive syntax is used for the activation of multiple transfers from a single test and this will be described in the sub-graph section. To specify a control flow from the test, the name of the test itself is used:

        test1 : x : y : e;

This makes x and then y active in parallel with d as specified in the previous statement, since d also follows 'test1' and precedes e;

5.1.6.6 Simple subgraphs

In the test operations previously described, the only operation carried out upon the success or failure of that test was a single data transfer. It is possible to activate a set of inter-related operations, termed a subgraph (analogous with a program block in structured programming languages). The single transfer activated previously is one example of a simple subgraph. A simple subgraph may either be the name of a transfer or the name of another test. This allows for the convenient nesting of multiple tests and their actions:

```
        if(test1)
                then if(test2)
                        then action1;
                        else action2;
                else while(test3)
                        do action3;
```

In this example, in each of the tests shown, the text following specifies a simple subgraph, some of which take the form of further nested
tests with their own nested subgraphs.

5.1.6.7 Complex subgraphs

The concept of the subgraph is taken further by its extension to allow pendent control sequencing of arbitrary complexity in the form of
complex subgraphs. A complex subgraph has exactly the same syntax as
the main graph but with the preamble removed (i.e. it operates in the
same data domain as the main graph and does not have its own input and
output ports). The complex subgraph is delimited by braces and has
its own unique start and end nodes:

```
while(test) do {
        < : a : b,c : d : >
        a : e : f : d;
}
```

It should be noted that depending on the context in which this is
used, the closing brace might need to be followed by a statement terminator.

All the usual operators may be used within a complex subgraph, including further test operators. This allows multiple levels of nesting and arbitrarily complex subgraphs:

```
< : a :
if(test1) then {
                < : c,d : >;
        } else
                while(test2) do {
                        < : e : if(test3) then f else g : >
                }
        : h : >;
```

5.2 THE IMPLEMENT PROGRAM

The 'implement' program converts G descriptions to HDL descriptions. It first checks the existence of applicable switches (see appendix I) and then proceeds to convert the G description to an HDL description interactively unless interaction is turned off.

The status of the graph is checked for validity and determinacy, and the requirement for a hardware implementation. The parts of the specification which were meaningless at level 1 are then checked, namely the initialisation information for the cells against the cell sizes. If any inconsistency is found, the program aborts. Otherwise it proceeds to process the graph. The various parts of the data structure are cleared in case they were set by the validation software. For every data operator, the input cells are marked to the effect that they are read, and output cells that they are written. The test operators are marked as being for word or bit tests. At this point any non-functional cells can be removed from the description. The bit widths of the cells can then be ascertained by examining the subgraphs in the libraries. This is done by piping questions on the specifications stored in the library, and receiving answers back, using the 'quest' program. Any cells not in the library are made the default size, or the designer is asked to supply the size. The transfers to busses are then made tristate or open-collector, and the process of constructing the HDL description can begin.

This is a case of constructing the text output file so that it meets with the HDL language specifications. The 'defines' and 'includes' are put out, followed by the graph name. The simple data cells are listed as registers of the appropriate size. The non-simple cells, i.e. those which require increment, decrement, shift, clear, etc. can then be put out with the appropriate description and bit sizes. The data operators are then considered. All the defined data operators and self type data operators are listed. The data graph can then be constructed in HDL. This consists of constructing all the relevant transfer expressions. The names of the graph input and output cells are preceded by a '.' to distinguish them from internal cells. The straightforward connections are listed. The input transfers (always connected), the simple (predefined) transfers, and the output (named) transfers can then be completed. Assertions and tests complete the data graph. The control graph is unaltered at level 2 from its specification at level 1, and is thus put out unchanged.

The multiplier of figure 3.5 has been produced using the implement program.

CHAPTER 6

Integrated Circuit
Description Language and
Circuit Description Language

As an introduction to the second part of the chapter, this section introduces the notation used to describe the signals which must be applied to an integrated circuit in order to realise a desired operation. In a low level description, the operation of a circuit can be
described fully by listing the various outputs which occur for all the
possible input sequences. In reality, this is unmanageable and since,
in a design environment, it is much more informative to know the input
sequence which is required to produce a desired output condition, each
circuit description includes a list of all the possible operations
which can be performed, along with the relevant inputs. In order to
differentiate between the wide range of possible input signal sequences, it was necessary to develop a simple yet unambiguous notation
which can be used to specify a signal.

6.1   SIGNAL REPRESENTATIONS

Conventionally, the operation of a digital circuit may be described
with a waveform timing diagram. To specify completely the control se-

quence and define the operation of the internal circuitry fully, the waveform of every control pin must be included. Alternatively, the resulting waveform timing diagram may be represented textually by laboriously stating the level of every control signal during the smallest distinguishable time period. However, an examination of the waveform timing diagram would reveal that most of this textual information is redundant. In most cases, it is only necessary to note the changes in control signal levels and to list the levels of the associated inputs, before, during, and after that change has taken place. As a result, the following notation was primarily developed to illustrate signal levels and signal level changes during a small time period, but complete waveforms may be described as a sequence of these elementary signals.

6.1.1   Level signals

Many integrated circuits, especially combinational circuits, respond to level signals. For example, a simple code converter has one input port, one output port and a single control terminal 'g' which enables the output when it is high and disables it when it is low. The high level signal g, specified during period T and shown in figure 6.1, requires terminal g to be high during period T but places no restriction on terminal g before or after this period. Similarly, the low level signal !g, specified during period T and shown in figure 6.2, requires terminal g to be low during period T but places no restriction on terminal g before or after this time period.

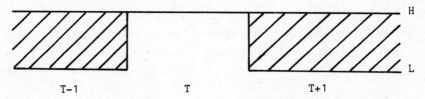

e.g. signal g during period T

FIG. 6.1.   High level signal

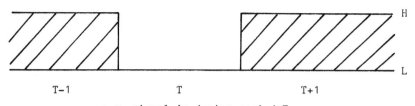

e.g. signal !g during period T

FIG. 6.2.   Low level signal

6.1.2   Edge signals

In many integrated circuits, it is a change in signal level, known as
an edge, which causes a particular operation to occur. For example, a
positive edge-triggered flip-flop transfers the data present at the
input port to the output port on the action of a positive edge at terminal ck. The signal sequence !ck, ck, specified during periods T and
T+1, implies that a positive edge occurs between period T and T+1 as
shown in figure 6.3. As this signal sequence is required in many circuit descriptions it is abbreviated to either ck+, specified during
period T, or +ck specified during period T+1.

> The positive leading edge signal +ck requires a positive edge
> to occur on terminal ck at the start of the specified time
> period. This signal requires terminal ck to be low prior to
> the specified time period and high during the specified time
> period.

> The positive lagging edge signal ck+ requires a positive edge
> to occur on terminal ck at the end of the specified time
> period. This signal requires terminal ck to be low during the
> specified time period and high after the specified time
> period.

114

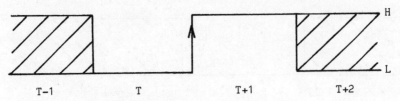

e.g. signal ck+ during period T or signal +ck during period T+1
FIG. 6.3.   Positive edge signal

Similarly, the signal sequence ck, !ck, specified during periods T and T+1 is abbreviated to either ck- specified during period T, or -ck specified during period T+1, as shown in figure 6.4. In addition the simplified signals +ck, ck+, -ck and ck- have the added advantage that they emphasise that an edge, as opposed to a level, causes the activation of the circuit.

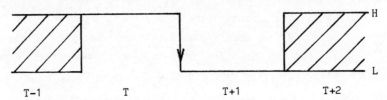

e.g. signal ck- during period T or signal -ck during period T+1
FIG. 6.4.   Negative edge signal

6.1.3   Pulse signals

Many integrated circuits respond to pulse signals. For example, a pulse triggered J-K master-slave flip-flop will, depending on the J and K inputs, change state by the application of positive pulses to terminal 'clock'. A positive pulse applied to terminal clock during period T can be described, using level signals, as !clock, clock, !clock, specified during periods T-1, T and T+1. This sequence can be abbreviated to +clock-, specified during period T, as shown in figure 6.5.

The positive pulse signal +clock- requires a positive pulse to occur on terminal clock during the specified time period. This signal requires terminal clock to be low prior to the specified time period, high during the specified time period, and low after the specified time period.

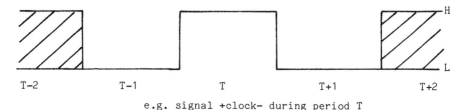

e.g. signal +clock- during period T

FIG. 6.5.   Positive pulse signal

Similarly, a negative pulse applied to terminal clock during period T can be represented by clock, !clock, clock, specified during periods T-1, T and T+1, and can be abbreviated to -clock+, specified during period T, as shown in figure 6.6. In addition, the simplified signals +clock- and -clock+ have the added advantage that they emphasise that a pulse, as opposed to a level, causes the activation of the circuit.

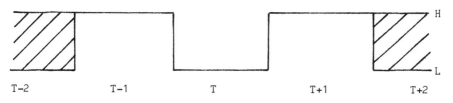

e.g. signal -clock+ during period T

FIG. 6.6.   Negative pulse signal

6.1.4   Expandable pulse signals

Figures 6.3, 6.4 and 6.5 have illustrated the notations used to represent level signals, edge signals and pulse signals. In general, an edge signal implies one change of signal level and a pulse signal implies two changes of signal level. However, as these simple edge

116

and pulse signals were too rigid to describe conveniently many of the commonly used integrated circuits, a more flexible class of pulse signal description had to be developed. For example, the output port of a transparent latch follows the data present at the input port while control terminal g is high and then this data is latched when terminal g goes low. At first glance, it would appear that the action associated with loading the latch could be fully described by the conventional positive pulse signal +g-. However, in many applications it is necessary to hold the enable terminal g high for more than one time period before latching the input, i.e. follow and hold. To achieve this, the load signal +g- has to be specified during consecutive time periods. This is impossible as +g-, specified during period T, requires a high level to be applied to terminal g during period T, and +g-, specified during period T+1, requires a low level to be applied to terminal g during the same time period. To overcome this and similar problems, four types of expandable pulse signals were introduced.

The positive leading and lagging expandable pulse signal /g\, shown in figure 6.7, requires a positive pulse to occur on terminal g during the specified time period. This signal requires terminal g to be low prior to the specified time period, high during the specified time period, and low after the specified time period. However, in order to increase the width of the positive pulse, /g\ may be followed by another signal involving a positive leading expandable pulse, i.e. /g\ or /g-.

The positive leading expandable pulse signal /g-, shown in figure 6.8, requires a positive pulse to occur on terminal g during the specified time period. This signal requires terminal g to be low prior to the specified time period, high during the specified time period, and low after the specified time period.

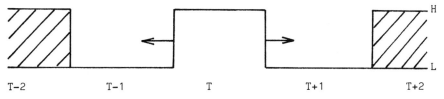

e.g. signal /g\ during period T

FIG. 6.7.   Positive leading and lagging expandable pulse signal

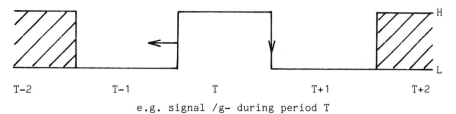

e.g. signal /g- during period T

FIG. 6.8.   Positive leading expandable pulse signal

Similarly, the negative leading and lagging expandable pulse signal
\g/, and the negative leading expandable pulse signal \g+, for terminal g, are shown in figures 6.9 and 6.10 respectively.   In the case of
the expandable pulse signals /g\, /g-, \g/ and \g+:

A '/' is a less rigid form of a '+' in +g- or -g+.

A '\' is a less rigid form of a '-' in +g- or -g+

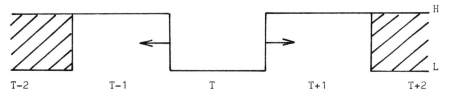

e.g. signal \g/ during period T

FIG. 6.9.   Negative leading and lagging expandable pulse signal

118

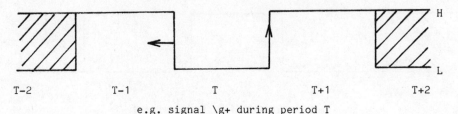

T-2   T-1   T   T+1   T+2

e.g. signal \g+ during period T

FIG. 6.10.   Negative leading expandable pulse signal

The horizontal arrow, shown in the expandable pulse diagrams, indicates that the pulse width is expandable in the direction of the arrow. An expandable pulse, shown with an arrow pointing to the right,
which is specified during period T may have its width expanded providing that it is followed by an expandable pulse, shown with an arrow
pointing to the left, during period T+1. For example:

           /g\ can be expanded with /g\ or /g-
           \g/ can be expanded with \g/ or \g+

If the expandable pulse, shown with an arrow pointing to the right,
is not followed by another expandable pulse, shown with an arrow
pointing to the left, then the '/' or '\' is replaced by its rigid
counterpart '+' or '-'.

6.1.5   Signal representations with timing constraints

Normally, the basic time period in which a signal is active is fixed
for a particular design but the individual level, edge and pulse signals can carry local timing constraints. This information is used to
specify detailed timing information such as setup and hold times and
is necessary to ensure that the data and steering control inputs are
stable for the required time before and/or after an edge or clocking
signal. A timing constraint may be attached either to the beginning
or to the end of the time period in which a signal is specified but,
as an edge signal can only occur on a period boundary, no timing in-

formation may be associated with it. For example, the high level signal a{p/q :r/s}, shown in figure 6.11 and specified during period T,
requires terminal a to be high for at least p ns before the start of
period T, high during all of period T and high for at least s ns after
the end of period T. The two additional timing constraints, q and r,
ensure that the width of period T is greater than both q and r ns. If
a timing constraint is prefixed by a colon (':') it applies to the end
of the time period, otherwise it applies to the start of the time
period, giving:

    p   the setup time for the start of the time period.
    q   the hold time for the start of the time period.
    r   the setup time for the end of the time period.
    s   the hold time for the end of the time period.

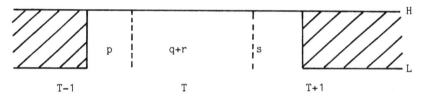

e.g. signal a{p/q:r/s} during period T

FIG. 6.11.   Level signal with leading and lagging constraints

The values of p, q, r and s may be positive, negative or zero providing that the width of the active region is positive. The high level signal a{p/q}, shown in figure 6.12 and specified during period T,
is a special case of the general signal a{p/q:q/r} and requires terminal a to be high for at least p ns before the start of period T and
remain high for at least q ns after the start of period T. Similarly,
the high level signal a{:r/s}, shown in figure 6.13 and specified during period T, requires terminal a to be high for at least r ns before
the end of period T and for at least s ns after the end of period T.

120

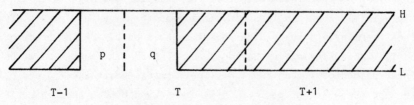

e.g. signal a{p/q} during period T

FIG. 6.12.   Level signal with leading constraints

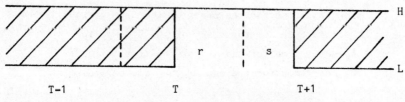

e.g. signal a{:r/s} during period T

FIG. 6.13.   Level signal with lagging constraints

Timing constraints may be added to either the beginning or the end
of level and pulse signals or to the inactive part of an edge signal
to produce the following 40 signal representations:

a	a{p/q :r/s}	a{p/q}	a{:r/s}
!a	!a{p/q :r/s}	!a{p/q}	!a{:r/s}
+a	+a{:r/s}		
a+	a+{p/q}		
-a	-a{:r/s}		
a-	a-{p/q}		
+a-	+a-{p/q :r/s}	+a-{p/q}	+a-{:r/s}
-a+	-a+{p/q :r/s}	-a+{p/q}	-a+{:r/s}
/a\	/a\{p/q :r/s}	/a\{p/q}	/a\{:r/s}
/a-	/a-{p/q :r/s}	/a-{p/q}	/a-{:r/s}
\a/	\a/{p/q :r/s}	\a/{p/q}	\a/{:r/s}
\a+	\a+{p/q :r/s}	\a+{p/q}	\a+{:r/s}

6.2   SIGNAL EXPRESSIONS

In order to describe the operation of an integrated circuit, a literal in a conventional boolean expression may be replaced by any one of the 40 signal representations to produce a signal expression. However, as the symbol '+' is used in the definition of a signal and the symbol '.' is used as a name extension operator, the following convention has been adopted:

      & represents the logical AND operator.

      ¦ represents the logical OR operator.

      ! represents the NEGATE operator.

In addition, as the NEGATE operator and a low true signal both use the same operator '!', round brackets ('(' and ')') must be used to distinguish a low true signal from the negation of a high true signal. For example

      !a and (!a) are low true signals.

      !(a) is the negation of a high true signal.

      !!a and !(!a) are the negation of low true signals.

The signal expression:

      a ¦ b{2/1} & +c

specified during period T, states that at least one of the following two conditions must be satisfied:

1) terminal a must be high during period T.

2) terminal b must be high for 2 ns before the start of period T and remain high for at least 3 ns. Terminal c must change from a low level to a high level at the start of period T.

A program, called reduce, can simplify a signal expression and produce the associated sum of products form which is simply the sum of
the prime implicants in the case of a signal expression containing
only basic level signals. This simplification process is achieved by
producing a sum of products, simplifying the products and finally
reducing the sums. The product terms involved in the simplification
process need not be identical but they must be compatible. For example:

```
+a & a- = +a-
+a & a{:1/2} = +a{:1/2}
+a & -a - 0
+a & a{1/2} = 0
```

However, as each product represents an alternative signal sequence,
the signal representations must be identical before the sums can be
reduced. For example, although logically

```
a ¦ a & b = a
```

the expression:

```
+a ¦ a & b
```

cannot be reduced because, for a given application, a & b might be a
less strict condition than +a. The complete product table for the
basic signal representations is given in figure 6.14.

&	a	!a	+a	a+	-a	a-	+a-	-a+	/a\	/a-	\a/	\a+
a	a	0	+a	0	0	a-	+a-	0	/a\	/a-	0	0
!a	0	!a	0	a+	-a	0	0	-a+	0	0	\a/	\a+
+a	+a	0	+a	0	0	+a-	+a-	0	+a\	+a-	0	0
a+	0	a+	0	a+	-a+	0	0	-a+	0	0	\a+	\a+
-a	0	-a	0	-a+	-a	0	0	-a+	0	0	-a/	-a+
a-	a-	0	+a-	0	0	a-	+a-	0	/a-	/a-	0	0
+a-	+a-	0	+a-	0	0	+a-	+a-	0	+a-	+a-	0	0
-a+	0	-a+	0	-a+	-a+	0	0	-a+	0	0	-a+	-a+
/a\	/a\	0	+a\	0	0	/a-	+a-	0	/a\	/a-	0	0
/a-	/a-	0	+a-	0	0	/a-	+a-	0	/a-	/a-	0	0
\a/	0	\a/	0	\a+	-a/	0	0	-a+	0	0	\a/	\a+
\a+	0	\a+	0	\a+	-a+	0	0	-a+	0	0	\a+	\a+

FIG. 6.14.   AND table for basic signal types

6.2.1   Signal representations with multiple timing constraints

Many of the integrated circuits which are in common use are members of a family of functionally identical units (e.g. the SN74163 and SN74S163). Providing each family member is pin compatible, one integrated circuit description may be used to describe all the family members. This reduces the amount of textual information which is needed to describe a large family group and simplifies the task of adding new integrated circuits to the library. In the Texas Instruments TTL data book the following symbols are used to identify the individual family members:

    O = Ordinary
    L = Low power
    LS = Low Power Schottky
    S = Schottky
    H = High Power

124

The syntax of the signal expressions can accommodate alternative sets of timing constraints and each constraint applies to an individual circuit option. In addition, the signal expression simplification program, reduce, can handle signals and signal expressions with multiple timing constraints. This program can be used to simplify a signal expression involving multiple timing constraints or to select a specific signal expression from a general signal expression with multiple timing constraints. For example the general signal expression for the O and L options can be simplified:

$$z\{O, L = 1/2, 3/4\} \ \& \ z\{O = 4/1\} \Rightarrow z\{O, L = 4/2, 3/4\}$$

or the specific signal expression for the O option can be selected:

$$z\{O, L = 1/2, 3/4\} \ \& \ z\{O = 4/1\} * O \Rightarrow z\{4/2\}$$

6.2.2 Net signal for the present time period

A program, called 'follow', is used to construct the control signals which are required to realise a sequence of signal expressions. For example, if one of the signal representations is specified during period T-1 it limits the choice of signal which can be specified during period T. Follow is used to test the compatibility of two consecutive signals and to generate the net signal for the present time period, from the past and present signals. For example, signal a, specified during period T-1, followed by signal !a, specified during period T, forms a compatible sequence and produces the net signal -a for period T. The following three additional signal representations are used to supplement the 40 basic signals previously introduced.

1) Signal 0 indicates that the past and present signal are incompatible. For example, signal a+ followed by signal -a generates signal 0.

2) Signal 1 indicates that the basic past and present signals

(i.e. signals with their timing constraints removed) are compatible but their timing constraints are incompatible. For example, signal a followed by signal !a generates signal -a, but
signal a{:1/2} followed by signal !a generates signal 1.

3) Signal 2 is used to indicate the don't care condition. For
example, signal a+ followed by signal 2 generates signal +a.

	a	!a	+a	a+	-a	a-	+a-	-a+	/a\	/a-	\a/	\a+	2
a	a	-a	0	-a+	-a	a-	0	-a+	0	0	-a/	-a+	2
!a	+a	!a	+a	a+	0	+a-	+a-	0	+a\	+a-	0	0	2
+a	a	-a	0	-a+	-a	a-	0	-a+	0	0	-a/	-a+	2
a+	+a	0	+a	0	0	+a-	+a-	0	+a\	+a-	0	0	+a
-a	+a	!a	+a	a+	0	+a-	+a-	0	+a\	+a-	0	0	2
a-	0	-a	0	-a+	-a	0	0	-a+	0	0	-a/	-a+	-a
+a-	0	-a	0	-a+	-a	0	0	-a+	0	0	-a/	-a+	-a
-a+	+a	0	+a	0	0	+a-	+a-	0	+a\	+a-	0	0	+a
/a\	0	-a	0	-a+	-a	0	0	-a+	a\	a-	-a/	-a+	-a
/a-	0	-a	0	-a+	-a	0	0	-a+	0	0	-a/	-a+	-a
\a/	+a	0	+a	0	0	+a-	+a-	0	+a\	+a-	a/	a+	+a
\a+	+a	0	+a	0	0	+a-	+a-	0	+a\	+a-	0	0	+a
2	a	!a	+a	a+	-a	a-	+a-	-a+	/a\	/a-	\a/	\a+	2

FIG. 6.15. Net present signal table for basic signal types

A table stating the net present period signals, generated from all
the combinations of past and present period signals, is given in figure 6.15. This table includes the don't care signal (i.e. 2) as well
as the 12 basic signals. In addition, there are two additional entries
in the table which are not signals but they can be produced as follows:

1) Signal /a\ followed by signal /a\ generates an intermediate
signal a\.

126

 2) Signal \a/ followed by signal \a/ generates an intermediate
 signal a/.

Although there are no signals directly corresponding to a\ and a/,
they behave in a similar manner to /a\ and \a/ when calculating the
net present period signal. Figure 6.16 illustrates a sequence of signals which cannot be directly implemented. If the sequence !a{0/4},
+a-, 2, 2, specified during periods T, T+1, T+2 and T+3, is to be re-
expressed using level signals based on a 3 unit time period, a level
clash appears during period T+1. Assuming a don't care condition for
period T-1, then the signal levels are as follows:

 The net signal for period T is signal 2 followed by signal
 !a{0/4} giving signal !a{0/4}.

 The net signal for period T is signal !a{0/4} followed by signal +a- giving signal 1.

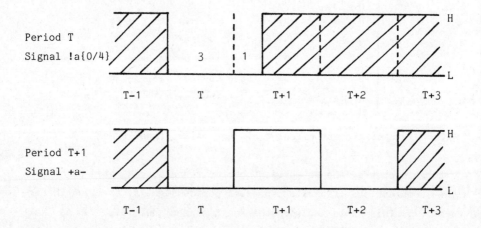

FIG. 6.16.   Incompatible signal sequence

If a time period of 3 micro seconds is used, the signal +a- cannot be
specified during the time period immediately after signal !a{0/4} has
been specified. This problem can be easily solved as shown below.

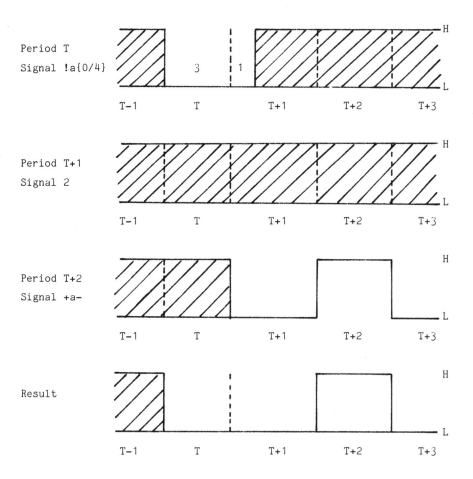

FIG. 6.17.   Don't care signal added to an incompatible sequence

As shown in figure 6.17, a don't care condition must be inserted
between signals !a{0/4} and +a- and all the signals which occur after
!a{0/4} are delayed by one time period. The new control sequence can
then be re-expressed as follows:

    The net signal for period T is signal 2 followed by signal
    !a{0/4} giving signal !a{0/4}.

The net signal for period T+1 is signal !a{0/4} followed by signal 2 giving signal !a{0/1}.

The net signal for period T+2 is signal !a{0/1} followed by signal +a- giving signal +a-.

The net signal for period T+3 is signal +a- followed by signal 2 giving signal -a.

The net signal for period T+4 is signal -a followed by signal 2 giving signal 2.

Therefore, in order to implement the signal sequence !a{0/4}, +a-, 2, 2, specified during periods T, T+1, T+2 and T+3, using a regular 3 micro second time period, the level signal sequence !a, !a, a, !a, 2 is required during time periods T, T+1, T+2 and T+3.

6.3   THE INTEGRATED CIRCUIT DESCRIPTION LANGUAGE ICDL

A program, called icdl, has been written to check that an ICDL description is plausible and to install it into the integrated circuit database. The mechanics of this program, and the operation of the library system, are described elsewhere [28]. This section is only concerned with explaining the syntax and semantic interpretation of the language.   However, it is worth noting that as the ICDL parser is two pass, it produces meaningful error messages, and does not suffer from any forward reference problems.   ICDL is capable of describing any family of digital integrated circuits but for convenience the examples given in this chapter are taken from the Texas Instruments TTL Data Book [31]. Extensive use is made of the signal types and complex expressions described previously.

6.4   THE ICDL PROGRAM LAYOUT

The ICDL verification program is two pass, and does not suffer from any forward reference problems. However, in order to standardise the layout of all the ICDL programs in the library, the following order of declarations must be observed:

```
integrated circuit name
{
            attribute declarations
            default declarations
            macro declarations
            port declaration
            bus declarations
            pin declarations
            expansion algorithms
}
```

The main body of the ICDL program must be surrounded by braces ('{' and '}') and must follow the integrated circuit name which declares the circuit options and the number of functional elements in the associated ICDL description.

6.4.1 Integrated circuit name

Each ICDL description must include the name of the integrated circuit family and give a list of the individual options which are available. The integrated circuit name SN7400[O,L,LS,S,H] is used to represent the integrated circuits: SN7400, SN74L00, SN74LS00, SN74S00 and SN74H00. This name implies that the information for all five SN7400 family members will be given in the associated ICDL description.

6.4.2 Attribute declarations

The attributes of an integrated circuit must be listed in the ICDL description, the keyword 'TYPE' being used to identify the attribute list. These attributes enable the integrated circuit library search program 'attribute', to select a few integrated circuits which are possible candidates for a given application. The design programs can then interrogate these selected ICDL descriptions in detail to find the most suitable circuit. The declaration:

TYPE counter, up, down, binary, bit = 4 ;

declares a 4-bit up/down binary counter.

The declaration:

TYPE rom, bit = 4, word = 1024 ;

declares a 1K x 4-bit ROM.

The keyword 'word' is exclusively used for the number of words in an integrated circuit. For example, the number of words in a memory. Similarly the keyword 'element' may be used to indicate how many discrete functional elements there are on the chip. For example, the number of gates in a pack. The keyword 'bit' is much more general purpose and can be used to represent the number of bits (e.g. the number of bits in a counter), or the number of inputs (e.g. the number of inputs to a logic gate).

These three keywords are the only ones which may take a numeric argument (assignment). All other arguments must be simple 'buzzwords'. If a word in the attribute list is not known to the system then the ICDL program will ask the user if they wish it to be inserted (assuming that interaction is enabled, which it is by default). If the user wishes to find out all the recognisable 'buzzwords' then these can be listed by using the 'attribute' program.

6.4.3   Default declarations

Associated with every terminal declaration (as will be described

later) it is possible to have declarations of certain physical constraints (timing and electrical characteristics). These constraints
rarely vary from pin to pin especially when a number of pins form a
logical grouping (port) and thus a mechanism has been included for defining 'default' values which the system will assume apply in the absence of a specific declaration tied to an object. The default declaration facility is available for SPEED, DRIVE, LOAD and WIDTH information. The syntax and interpretation of each of these is the same
as would be used within the body of an object declaration and will be
described in the appropriate sections.

Default SPEED, DRIVE and LOAD declarations must appear immediately
after the optional attribute declaration. Failure to include a SPEED,
DRIVE or LOAD declaration for any of the circuit options present in
the integrated circuit name results in the appropriate error message.
A WIDTH declaration may also appear in this part of the ICDL description. However, if no WIDTH declaration is given, the width for all the
circuit options is assumed to be infinitesimal.

6.4.4   Terminal declarations

The ICDL description defines how an integrated circuit can be considered as a simple blackbox with terminals. These logical terminals
may carry a single signal (a pin) or have multiple lines (a port) or
perform a specific function (a macro).

In order to explain the complex operation of an integrated circuit,
the function of each terminal must be fully declared. Therefore, the
bulk of the ICDL description consists of a list of the pins which are
associated with the actual integrated circuit and a list of the ports
which are associated with the conceptual blackbox. All these declarations must end with a semi-colon (';'), and a space, tab or newline
character may be used to delimit strings of characters. The names
which appear in the ICDL description may be constructed from upper
case letters, lower case letters, digits and the underscore ('_'),

132

providing that the following simple convention is obeyed:

1) Data book pin names must not start with a capital letter.

2) Blackbox terminal names must start with a capital letter.

3) Keywords must be constructed using capital letters only.

6.4.5 Pin declarations

The ICDL description must include a list of all the pins which have an internal connection. Each pin declaration must include the name, type and number of the pin. The name and number of the pin are those given in the data book.

A pin which is associated with a port may be of one of the following types:

```
input(I),
output(O),
address(A),
function(F),
bus(B)
```

A pin of one of these types is declared by relating it to the appropriate bit in the relevant port (the syntax of a port descriptor is given in a later section). Pins which do not fall into this category may be one of three other types:

```
control pin
power supply
not connected
```

Some examples will help to make these distinctions clear:

        PIN 1 = a , I[1]<0> ;

declares pin 1 to be an input pin with name 'a' corresponding   to   bit
'0' on input port 1. Pins of other port types may be declared in a
similar manner:

        PIN 2 = b , O[2]<1> ;
        PIN 3 = c , A[1]<4> ;
        PIN 4 = d , F[2]<0> ;
        PIN 5 = e , B[1]<3> ;

The remaining pin types are declared similarly.

        PIN 6 = vcc ,VCC ;
        PIN 7 = f ;
        PIN 8 NC ;

where pin 6, known by the name 'vcc', is a power supply pin
corresponding to 'VCC' (ground is signified by using the string
'GND'), pin 7 is a control pin called 'f' and pin 8 has no internal
connection (NC). The ICDL verification program, icdl, will detect an
error if two pins are declared with the same name   or   number,   or   if
more than one pin is associated with the same bit in a port.

The examples shown so far have declared high true pins.   However,
four different types of pin name declarations are available by preceding the name itself by a character giving the 'sense' of the pin. This
character may be one from the set:

          High True (default)
    !   Low True
    +   Positive Edge triggered
    −   Negative Edge triggered

In use these would look like:

```
PIN 9 = g , I[2]<0> ;
PIN 10 = !h , O[3]<0> ;
PIN 11 = +pr;
```

and hence pin 9 is a high true input pin 'g', pin 10 is a low true
output pin 'h' and pin 11 is a positive edge triggered control pin
'pr'. These declarations may be made as and when required providing
that there are no intra-port conflicts:

```
PIN 12 = i , A[2]<0> ;
PIN 13 = !j , A[2]<1> ;
```

These declarations are inconsistent because address port 2 is thus declared to be both high and low true.

6.4.6 Port declarations

The ICDL description must include a list of all the input, output, address and function ports which are used in the pin declarations. A
port is identified by its type and number which must be unique. The
number of bits defines the width of the port and all the pins which
are assigned to that port must lie within the port width.

Associated with every port is an 'action' which defines how and when
the port is enabled. The port action is a complex expression constructed from data book pin names and macro names. However, the precise interpretation depends on the types of names which are used in
the expression.

> 1) A data book pin name may be used to construct any of the 12
> basic signal types introduced earlier. The resulting signal
> may appear with or without timing constraints but it may not
> appear in complement form.

2) A macro name may appear with or without timing constraints but it may not appear in complement form.

The port action specifies the signals which must be present in order to transfer data into an input, address or function port or to transfer data from an output port. The port declaration:

```
PORT I[1]<4> = a+ & b ;
```

declares input port I[1] to be 4 bits wide. Data is transferred into this port when terminal b is high and terminal a receives a positive edge. The port declaration:

```
PORT O[2]<4> = 1 ;
```

declares output port O[2] to be 4 bits wide. Data can always be transferred from this port as it is always enabled (action is 1).

A port declaration may include a list of associated macros. These macros take the same form as the more general macro facility which will be described later. When declared in this form, however, they are directly associated with a particular port and can be given the same constraints as are applied to the port. This feature is most often used when declaring complex function ports and this is how they will be named in the remainder of the chapter. The function port declaration:

```
PORT F[1]<4> =
{
Add    = !s0 & !s1 & !s2 & !s3 ;
Subtr  =  s0 & !s1 & !s2 & !s3 ;
And    = !s0 &  s1 & !s2 & !s3 ;
Or     =  s0 &  s1 & !s2 & !s3 ;
etc.
} ;
```

associated with the set of pins:

```
PIN 3 = s0 , F[1]<0> ;
PIN 4 = s1 , F[1]<1> ;
PIN 5 = s2 , F[1]<2> ;
PIN 6 = s3 , F[1]<3> ;
```

defines the macros which are associated with function port F[1].

6.4.7   Bus declarations

The ICDL description may include a list of bus declarations. A bus is a collection of pins which are associated with more than one port. A bus is identified by its number which must be unique. The width of the bus is equal to the width of the associated ports. In addition, all the ports which are associated with a bus must have identical bit widths.

The declarations:

```
PORT I[1]<4> = Write ;
PORT O[1]<4> = Read ;
BUS B[1] = I[1] / O[1] ;
```

give an example of a 4-bit input/output bus. The port declarations given show how bus B[1] can be used as an input port enabled by macro Write, or as an output port enabled by macro Read. When declaring the pins on a chip, those pins which are associated with a bus must be explicitly declared as being bits in the bus port and not declared as being bits in one of the constituent ports:

```
PIN 1 = a , B[1]<0>;
```

6.4.8   Macro declarations

The ICDL description may include a list of macros. A macro is defined in order to collect together in the form of a complex expression those actions which must occur in order to carry out some specific function on or with a chip. For example,

        Shiftr = s0 & !s1 & clk+ ;

defines a macro 'Shiftr'(shift-right) which is activated by ensuring that pin 's0' is high, pin 's1' is low and that at the end of the period the pin 'clk' has a positive edge applied (goes from low to high).

The macro name may be constructed from letters, digits and the underscore '_', providing it starts with a capital letter. The macro action is a complex expression constructed from data book pin names and macro names. However, the precise interpretation depends on the types of names which are used in the expression:

> 1) A data book pin name may be used to construct any of the basic signal types. The resulting signal may appear with or without timing constraints but it may not appear in complement form.

> 2) A macro name may appear with or without timing constraints but it may not appear in complement form.

A timing constraint applied to a macro effectively causes a timing constraint to be applied to a subexpression.

The two macros:

        Enable = a & b{0 = 2/1} ;
        Load = Enable{0 = 1/1} & +c ;

cause a timing constraint to be applied to a subexpression as macro
Load is given by:

Load = (a & b{0 = 2/1}){0 = 1/1} & +c

which produces the following overall complex expression for control
terminal Load:

Load = a{0 = 1/1} & b{0 = 3/2} & +c

The complement of a macro or signal type cannot appear in an action
because the complement merely states what signals must not occur and
does not explicitly state what signals must occur. The macro declaration:

Enable = !Clr & I[1];

is illegal since although the macro simply states that the enable
function is active provided that there is data at input port one and
the 'Clr' function is disabled it does not state how the 'Clr' function may be disabled and there may be many ways of doing this.

It is not permissible to declare macros which are defined in terms
of themselves. The ICDL verification program uses Warshall's Algorithm to generate the transitive closure of the Boolean connectivity
matrix representing the system of macros. The transitive closure
shows the existence of paths between elements in a system and a macro
is defined in terms of itself if the leading diagonal of the transitive closure matrix has a non zero entry - in other words, if there is
a path of any length from a macro to itself.

The system of macros:

```
Read = A & b ;
A = C & d ;
C = Read & e ;
```

is not permissible because the macros Read, A and C are all defined in terms of themselves. An expansion of the macro C in to its constituent parts shows this:

```
C = Read & e;
C = (A & b) & e;
C = ((C & d) & b) & e;
C = C & d & b & e;
```

6.5   INFORMATION ASSOCIATED WITH THE DECLARATIONS

It is now appropriate to introduce the various types of additional information which can be attached to the pin, port and macro declarations previously described. As much of this information is only applicable to certain types of declarations, specific application details will be given in the appropriate sections. However, the following general rules must be obeyed:

1) No additional information can be added to a bus declaration.

2) Additional information intended for an input, output, address or function pin must be added to the appropriate port and therefore applies to all the pins in that port.

3) Additional information added to a function port applies to all the macros which are associated with the port.

4) It is illegal to attach more than one similar piece of ad-

140

ditional information to any individual declaration.

6.5.1 Conditional expressions

A conditional expression is used to state when a particular operation
can or cannot occur. It may be associated with a control pin, macro or
port declaration. A conditional expression is a complex expression
constructed from data book pin names, macro names or port names. However, the precise interpretation depends on the types of names used in
the expression.

> 1) A data book pin name may be used to construct any of the
> basic signal types. The resulting signal may appear, with or
> without timing constraints, in true or complement form.   The
> truth of a signal means that the condition applies when that
> signal is present and the complement of a signal means that
> the condition applies when the complement of that signal is
> present.

> 2) A macro name may appear, with or without timing con-
> straints, in true or complement form. The truth of a macro
> name means that the condition applies when that macro is en-
> abled and the complement of a macro name means that the condi-
> tion applies when that macro is not enabled.

> 3) A port name may appear, with or without timing constraints,
> in true or complement form. The truth of a port name means
> that the condition applies when data is present at that port
> and the complement of a port name means that the condition ap-
> plies when data is not present at that port.

The conditional expression:

    !m & !Read & I[1]

means that the condition applies during the time period in which:

    1) Pin m is low.

    2) Macro Read is not enabled.

    3) Input port I[1] has the appropriate data.

The more complex conditional expression:

    +m & Read & I[1]{0 = 1/2}

means that the condition applies during any time period when:

    1) Pin m receives a positive edge at the start of the time period.

    2) Macro Read is enabled.

    3) In the case of circuit option O:
Input port I[1] has the appropriate data for at least 1 time unit before the start of period T and for at least 2 time units after the start of that period.

    4) In the case of any option other than O:
Input port I[1] has the appropriate data.

6.5.2 Automatic conditional expressions

In a large integrated circuit description many of the port and macro actions are interrelated. As a result, conditions which are associated with these ports and macros are very similar. In an attempt to reduce the amount of repetitive textual information in a large integrated circuit description with many interrelated port and macro actions, two other forms of expression were introduced:

       ?
       ??

For brevity, all the examples given in this section will concentrate on the automatic VALID condition. However, other conditions can be dealt with in a similar manner.

The three declarations:

```
R   = p : VALID = a ;
Rd = q : VALID = b ;
Read = R & Rd ;
```

define 3 interrelated macros. Macro R is valid when signal a is present, macro Rd is valid when signal b is present but macro Read is always valid as

```
VALID = 1
```

is the default VALID condition. However, this is not a realistic example because macro Read is almost certainly subject to the VALID conditions declared for macros R and Rd.

If macro Read is subject to these VALID conditions it can be more conveniently declared as:

```
Read = R & Rd : VALID = ? ;
```

The true VALID condition for macro Read is generated automatically by including the VALID conditions for each of the signals and macros appearing in its action.

```
VALID(Read) = ((VALID(R))&R)&((VALID(Rd)&Rd)
            = ((a) & R) & ((b) & Rd)
            = a & b & R & Rd
```

Substituting for the macro actions generates:

VALID(Read) = a & b & (p) & (q)
            = a & b & c & d

Therefore, the macro declaration:

Read = R & Rd : VALID = ? ;

automatically produces the macro declaration:

Read = R & Rd : VALID = a & b & p & q ;

Finally, as all the macros involved in the action are replaced by their own individual actions, the macro declaration becomes:

Read = p & q : VALID = p & q & a & b ;

Thus, the automatic conditional expression, VALID = ?, generates the actual VALID condition for macro Read by using the VALID conditions associated with all the macros and signals which appear in the recursive simplification of the original action.

The automatic conditional expression, VALID = ??, also generates the conditional expression associated with a macro or port action but instead of using the VALID conditions associated with the macros which appear in the recursive simplification of the original action, it uses the VALID conditions associated with the final signals.

The declarations:

```
R  = p : VALID = a ;
Rd = q : VALID = b;
Read = R & Rd : VALID = ?? ;
PIN 1 = p : VALID = aa ;
PIN 2 = q : VALID = bb ;
```

give an example of the VALID = ?? expression. The VALID condition for
macro Read is generated automatically by simplifying Read to produce
the individual signal types and then inserting the appropriate VALID
conditions.

```
Read = R & Rd
     = (p) & (q)
     = p & q
VALID(Read) = ((VALID(p) & p) & ((VALID(q) & q)
     = ((aa) & p) & ((bb) & q)
     = p & q & aa & bb
```

There is no limit to the number of automatic conditions which can appear in an ICDL description but it is obviously meaningless to attach
an automatic condition directly to a control pin declaration.

   The full power of the automatic conditions is realised when it is
applied directly to a function port declaration. For example, the declaration:

```
PORT F[1]<4> =
{
Add        = F0 & !m ;
Subtract   = F1 & !m ;
etc.
Complement = F0 & m ;
Shift_left = F1 & m ;
```

```
        etc.
        } : VALID = ? ;
```

associated with the macro declarations:

```
        F0 = !s0 & !s1 & !s2 & !s3 : VALID = A;
        F1 =  s0 & !s1 & !s2 & !s3 : VALID = B;
        etc.
```

applies automatic VALID conditions to all of the macros associated with the complex function port F[1] of an ALU.

6.5.3 Alternative action conditional expressions

The conditional expressions introduced so far have only been applied to a port or macro action with one mode of operation. However, some integrated circuits can be operated by alternative actions and it is possible for each individual action to have a separate conditional expression. For example, the declaration:

```
        Shift = !ck1&+ck2|+ck1&!ck2:VALID=!Load;
```

associated with a shift register, which has a parallel load facility, declares a macro with two modes of operation. Control terminal Shift can be enabled by applying a positive edge to one or other of the control pins, ck1 or ck2, while the other control pin is held low. Therefore, if macro Shift is enabled during any time period in which macro Load is not enabled, the design programs can select the action which is most convenient to implement. However, if the two control pins, ck1 and ck2, are not identical, it is possible that the two individual actions may have different VALID conditions. For example, their timing constraints may be different.

Assuming that the action !ck1 & +ck2 is valid when macro A is enabled and the action +ck1 & !ck2 is valid when macro B is enabled,

146

then the declaration:

```
Shift = !ck1&+ck2|+ck1&!ck2:VALID=A|B;
```

is not sufficient to define the operation of macro Shift because it merely states that both of the alternative actions are valid when either macro A or control terminal B is enabled. Therefore, if alternative port or macro actions have individual conditional expressions, the alternative actions must be included in the overall conditional expression. The declaration:

```
Shift = !ck1 & +ck2 | +ck1 & !ck2 :
VALID = !ck1 & +ck2 & A | +ck1 & !ck2 & B ;
```

declares a macro with two alternative actions and each action has an individual VALID condition.

6.5.4   Scope of a conditional expression

A conditional expression may be associated with a control pin, port or macro declaration. However, there are occasions when the control pin, port or macro is not subject to the given conditional expression and is assigned automatically to the default expression. The macro declaration:

```
Read = +a : VALID = A[1] ;
```

states that macro Read can only be enabled when data is present at the address port A[1]. However, macro Read may be disabled at any time. Therefore, !Read = !(+a) = !a is subject to the default VALID condition, VALID = 1.

The port declaration:

```
PORT I[1]<4> = +b- : VALID = Enable;
```

states that input port I[1] can only be enabled when macro Enable is enabled. However, input port I[1] may be disabled at any time. Therefore, it is subject to the default VALID condition, VALID = 1.

The control pin declaration:

>   PIN 1 = +c : VALID = d ;

states that control pin c can only be enabled (i.e changed from a low level to a high level) when pin d is high. However, any signal associated with pin c, which does not require a positive edge, can be enabled at any time. Therefore a signal not requiring a positive edge is subject to the default VALID condition, VALID = 1.

In general, if a conditional expression is associated with a control pin c, then depending on the type of signal which is applied, pin c is subject to either the given conditional expression or its default expression.

6.6   DECLARATION MODIFIERS

6.6.1   VALID Expression

A control pin, macro or port declaration may be able to produce its associated function only under certain strict conditions. To allow for this, a control pin, port or macro declaration can have an additional expression which states when its normal operation is valid. If no VALID expression is given the control pin, port or macro declaration is assigned the default expression, VALID = 1, i.e. the action is always valid.

The port declaration:

>   PORT O[1]<4> = Read : VALID = A[1] ;

is an example of a port declaration with a VALID condition. If this declaration is part of the description of a 4-bit ROM and O[1] represents the 4-bit output and A[1] represents the address lines, then output port O[1] can only be enabled when the address port A[1] has the correct data. It must be stressed that it is the port action, given by macro Read, which is subject to the VALID condition and not macro Read, which is declared elsewhere. Therefore, any condition associated directly with macro Read has no effect on the action of output port O[1].

The two declarations:

```
PIN 1 =  !pr : VALID = clr ;
PIN 2 = !clr : VALID =  pr ;
```

are examples of control pin declarations with VALID conditions. If these declarations are part of the description of a J-K master-slave flip-flop with preset and clear, and pin 1 represents the low true preset pin and pin 2 represents the low true clear pin, then these declarations state that preset may be enabled only when clear is not enabled and vice-versa. The two declarations:

```
Preset = !pr : VALID = !Clear  ;
Clear  = !clr : VALID = !Preset ;
```

are examples of macro declarations with VALID conditions. If the macros are associated with the following low true control pins:

```
PIN 1 =  !pr ;
PIN 2 = !clr ;
```

then these declarations are another way of expressing the declarations of the previous example.

The declaration:

```
PORT F[1]<4> =
{
Add     = !s0 & !s1 & !s2 & !s3 : VALID = I[1] & I[2] ;
Subtr   =  s0 & !s1 & !s2 & !s3 : VALID = I[1] & I[2] ;
And     = !s0 &  s1 & !s2 & !s3 : VALID = I[1] & I[2] ;
Or      =  s0 &  s1 & !s2 & !s3 : VALID = I[1] & I[2] ;
etc.
} ;
```

is an example of a function port declaration with a VALID condition.
If this declaration is part of the description of a 4-bit ALU and I[1]
and I[2] represent the two 4-bit input words, then any binary operation associated with function port F[1] is only valid when both input
words are present. The above macro port declaration can be more conveniently expressed as follows:

```
PORT F[1]<4> =
{
Add     = !s0 & !s1 & !s2 & !s3 ;
Subtr   =  s0 & !s1 & !s2 & !s3 ;
And     = !s0 &  s1 & !s2 & !s3 ;
Or      =  s0 &  s1 & !s2 & !s3 ;
etc.
} : VALID = I[1] & I[2] ;
```

In this case the VALID expression applies to each macro within the
macro port.

However, it is not permissible to attach more than one similar piece
of additional information to a control pin, port or macro declaration.
Therefore, the port declaration:

```
PORT O[1]<4> = Read : VALID = A[1] : VALID = A[1] ;
```

is illegal, despite the fact that the two VALID conditions are not contradictory. It is also illegal to have a similar piece of additional information explicitly and implicitly attached to a macro in a macro port. Therefore, the control terminal port declaration:

```
PORT F[1]<4> =
{
Add     = !s0 &  !s1 &  !s2 &  !s3 : VALID = I[1] & I[2] ;
Subtr   =  s0 &  !s1 &  !s2 &  !s3 : VALID = I[1] & I[2] ;
And     = !s0 &   s1 &  !s2 &  !s3 : VALID = I[1] & I[2] ;
Or      =  s0 &   s1 &  !s2 &  !s3 : VALID = I[1] & I[2] ;
etc.
} : VALID = I[1] & I[2] ;
```

is also illegal because the macros Add, Subtr, And and Or have effectively two VALID conditions.

6.6.2   OVERRIDE Expression

The function associated with a control pin, port or macro may be overridden by the action associated with another control pin, port or macro which is enabled at the same time. To allow for this, a control pin, port or macro declaration can have an additional expression which states when its normal operation is overridden. If no OVERRIDE expression is given, the control pin, port or macro is assigned the default expression, OVERRIDE = 0, i.e. the action is never overridden.

The declaration:

```
PORT I[2]<1> = Shift_left : OVERRIDE = Load ;
```

is an example of a port declaration with an OVERRIDE condition. If this declaration is part of the description of a bidirectional shift register and I[2] is the shift left serial input, then port I[2] is overridden by the action of macro Load. In this example, I[1] represents a 4-bit parallel input port and would be declared as follows:

    PORT I[1]<4> = Load ;

Load is a macro representing the action of input port I[1].

6.6.3 WAIT Expression

The control pin, port and macro actions which have been declared so far have only been subject to VALID and OVERRIDE conditions during the period in which the action is enabled. However, some of the more complex LSI circuits which are associated with microprocessors require conditions to be fulfilled before the specified action can take place. To allow for this, an additional expression states which operations or conditions must have occurred in period T-1 so that the specified action can take place as normal during period T. If no WAIT expression is given, the control pin, port or macro is given the default expression, WAIT = 0, i.e. the operation does not have to wait on any other operation or condition.

The declaration:

    I[1]<4> = Write : WAIT = A[1] : VALID = A[1] ;

is a simple example of an input port declaration with a WAIT condition. If this declaration is part of the description of a slow memory and I[1] represents the 4-bit input port and A[1] represents the address lines, then the WAIT condition ensures that the Write operation of input port I[1] can only take place after the address has been present for one entire time period. The additional VALID condition ensures that the address remains present throughout the period in which the Write operation takes place.

152

6.6.4 OUTPUT Type

The type of output, associated with an output port, must be given, otherwise the individual pins are assumed to have normal TTL outputs. The declaration:

        PORT O[1]<4> = a : OUTPUT = TTL ;

declares an output port consisting of 4 pins with normal TTL outputs. However, as the default output type is TTL, this declaration can be abbreviated to:

        PORT O[1]<4> = a ;

The declaration:

        PORT O[2]<4> = b : OUTPUT = TRI ;

declares an output port consisting of 4 pins with tristate outputs. The declaration:

        PORT O[3]<4> = c : OUTPUT = OC ;

declares an output port consisting of 4 pins with open collector outputs.

6.6.5 INITIAL Conditions

In order to ensure that the described integrated circuit functions correctly when only a few of its features are required, a control pin or an input, address or function port may be given initial conditions. However, the initial conditions do not restrict the interconnections which are explicitly made by the designer. If no initial condition is given, the control pin or input, address or function port is assigned the default initial condition, INITIAL = X (i.e. the don't care condition).

The declaration:

        PIN 1 = up_down : INITIAL = X ;

declares a high true pin, called up_down, with a don't care initial
condition.   Therefore, if pin 1 is unused it may be tied high or low.
However, as the default initial condition is X, this declaration can
be abbreviated to simply:

        PIN 1 = up_down ;

The declaration:

        PIN 2 = !clear : INITIAL = H ;

declares a low true pin, called clear, which must be tied high if it
is unused. The declaration:

        PORT A[1]<4> = 1 : INITIAL = L ;

declares an address port A[1] consisting of 4 pins which must be tied
low if they are unused.

6.6.6   WIDTH of Pulse

The minimum pulse width of a signal which can be effectively applied
to an input, address, function or control pin must be given. This information can be attached to a control pin or to an input, address or
function port, or to a macro declaration. The minimum pulse width
must be given for each option specified in the integrated circuit name
and for programming ease all pulse widths are quoted in nano-seconds.
If no minimum pulse width is given, the control pin or input, address

or function port or macro declaration is assigned the default minimum pulse width, WIDTH = 0, i.e. the pulse width required to activate the circuit is infinitesimal.

The declaration:

```
    PIN 1 = !clear : WIDTH O, L = 5, 6 ;
```

declares a low true control pin, called clear, which can be activated by any signal greater than the following pulse widths:

```
    Option O          5 ns
    Option L          6 ns
```

However, as most of the control, input, address and function pins which are associated with a particular integrated circuit have the same minimum pulse width requirements, the minimum pulse width may be declared at the beginning of the ICDL description and can be temporarily modified later if necessary.

The declarations:

```
    WIDTH O, L = 5, 6 ;
    Up   = up_down & +ck ;
    Down = !up_down & +ck ;
    PIN 1 = up_down ;
    PIN 2 = +ck : WIDTH O, L = 1, 2 ;
```

declare two control pins and two macros. The two control terminals, Up and Down, and the individual control pin up_down are subject to the following minimum pulse width restrictions:

```
    Option O          5 ns
    Option L          6 ns
```

The individual control pin ck is subject to the following modified minimum pulse width restriction:

Option O   1 ns
Option L   2 ns

6.6.7   SPEED of Operation

The maximum speed of operation must be stated for each of the options specified in the integrated circuit name. This corresponds to the maximum clock frequency which can be applied to the circuit and it is quoted in Megahertz. Although the maximum clock rate is declared for the entire circuit, individual operations are also subject to the local timing constraints and minimum pulse width restrictions.

The declaration:

SPEED O, L, LS, S, H = 35, 3, 45, 125, 50 ;

declares the maximum clock rate for each circuit option to be as follows:

Option O =   35 MHz
Option L =   3 MHz
Option LS =   45 MHz
Option S = 125 MHz
Option H =   50 MHz

6.6.8   DELAY in Propagation

The propagation delay from a change in input, address, function or control signal level to a change in output signal level may be specified for each output port in the integrated circuit description. The delay must be stated for both a high to low level change and a low to

high level change and corresponds to the propagation delays tPHL and
tPLH which are given in the Texas Instruments TTL Data Book. The propagation delay is required for each option specified in the integrated
circuit name and must be quoted in nano seconds. A DELAY expression
is a complex expression constructed from the control pin names, input,
address and function port names and macro names which cause the output
transition. However, signal types, port names and macro names must
not appear in complement form. Conventional timing constraints, associated with complex expressions, are simply replaced by the propagation delay times, tPHL and tPLH, to form a delay expression. However,
the delay times may be attached to either end of the time period
depending on the type of signal which is used. For example, a leading
edge signal can only have a propagation delay attached to the end of
the time period.

The declaration:

        PORT O[1]<4> = Enable
        : DELAY = I[1]{O = 40/40} ¦ Enable{O = 35/30} ;

gives an example of an output port with a DELAY expression for the O
circuit option. Assuming that this declaration is part of the description of a binary to BCD code converter and I[1] is the binary input,
O[1] is the BCD output and the conversion is selected by macro Enable,
then the propagation delays are as follows:

        Delay for high to low output change from Enable = 35 ns
        Delay for low to high output change from Enable = 30 ns
        Delay for high to low output change from I[1] = 40 ns
        Delay for low to high output change from I[1] = 40 ns

It must be stressed that a DELAY expression is merely a convenient way
of expressing delay times and no attempt is made to simplify a DELAY
expression.

6.6.9   DRIVE Capability

The output current must be given for each output port in the ICDL
description. The current for both high and low level outputs is required for each option specified in the integrated circuit name. This
corresponds to the currents, IOH and IOL, as given in the TI Data
Book. For consistency, both IOH and IOL are quoted in micro amps.
Currents which flow into terminals are given positive values and
currents which flow out of terminals are given negative values. The
declaration:

> PORT O[1]<4> = Write : DRIVE O, L = 16000 / -400, 3600 / -200
> ;

declares an output port consisting of 4 pins and each pin has the following output current capabilities:

> Option O   IOL = 16 mA   IOH = -0.4 mA
> Option O   IOL = 3.6 mA   IOH = -0.2 mA

However, as most of the output pins which are associated with a particular integrated circuit have the same output current capabilities,
the output current may be declared at the beginning of the ICDL
description (using a default DRIVE declaration) and can be temporarily
modified later if necessary.

The declarations:

> DRIVE LS, L = 8000 / -400, 20000 / -1000 ;
> PORT O[1]<4> = Write ;
> PORT O[2]<1> = 1 : DRIVE LS = 9000 / -500 ;

declare two output ports. The 4 pins associated with output port O[1]
have the following output current capabilities:

```
Option LS    IOL =  8 mA    IOH = -0.4 mA
Option S     IOL = 20 mA    IOH = -1.0 mA
```

The pin associated with output port O[2] has   the   following   modified
output current capability:

```
Option LS    IOL =  9 mA    IOH = -0.5 mA
Option S     IOL = 20 mA    IOH = -1.0 mA
```

6.6.10 LOAD Requirement

The input current must be given for each input,   address   or   function
port or control pin in the ICDL description. The current for both high
and low level inputs is required for each option specified in the   integrated circuit name. This corresponds to the currents, IIH and IIL,
which are given in the Data Book.   Both IIH and IIL are quoted in   micro amps. Currents which flow into terminals are given positive values
and currents which flow out of terminals are given negative values.

The declaration:

```
PORT I[1]<4> = Read : LOAD 0, L = -1600 / 40, -180 / 10 ;
```

declares an input port consisting of 4 pins each   with   the   following
input current requirements:

```
Option O    IIL = -1.60 mA    IIH = 0.04 mA
Option O    IIL = -0.18 mA    IIH = 0.01 mA
```

However, as most of the control, input, address or function pins which
are associated with a particular integrated circuit have the same input current requirements, the input current may be declared at the beginning of the ICDL description and can be temporarily modified later
if necessary.

The declarations:

```
LOAD LS, S = -400 / 20, -2000 / 50 ;
PORT I[1]<4> = Read ;
PIN 1 = clear : LOAD LS = - 500 / 30 ;
PIN 2 = a , I[1]<0> ;
PIN 3 = b , I[1]<1> ;
PIN 4 = c , I[1]<2> ;
PIN 5 = d , I[1]<3> ;
PIN 6 = enable ;
```

declare two control pins and one input port. The control pin enable and the 4 pins associated with input port I[1] have the following input current requirements:

```
Option LS   IIL = -0.4 mA   IIH = 0.02 mA
Option S    IIL = -2.0 mA   IIH = 0.05 mA
```

The control pin 'clear' has the following modified input current requirement:

```
Option LS   IIL = -0.5 mA   IIH = 0.03 mA
Option S    IIL = -2.0 mA   IIH = 0.05 mA
```

6.7   LANGUAGE EXTENSIONS

6.7.1   Integrated circuits with multiple elements

The pin names, macro names and port names which have been used so far are only capable of describing integrated circuits with one functional element, e.g. a 4 line to 1 line data selector. However, many of the integrated circuits which are in common use have more than one functional element, e.g. a dual 4 line to 1 line data selector. Therefore, the syntax of the pin names, macro names and port names was extended so that integrated circuits with multiple functional elements could be described concisely.

Macro names (e.g. Read), port names (e.g. O[1]) and bus names (e.g. B[1]) may have an occurrence number which defines the functional element that they represent but all data book pin names must be unique. However, if the occurrence number is omitted, the terminal name, port name or bus name is assumed to belong to functional element 1, i.e. the first functional element on the integrated circuit.

Examples of terminal names, port names and bus names which belong to functional element 1 are given below.

```
I[1]<0>  or  I[1].1<0>
Read     or  Read.1
I[1]     or  I[1].1
B[1]     or  B[1].1
```

It is illegal to use an occurrence number higher than that declared in the attribute list.

The declaration:

```
PORT O[1].1<4> = Read.1 ;
PORT O[1].2<4> = Read.2 ;
Read.1 = p;
Read.2 = q;
PIN 1 = p ;
PIN 2 = q ;
PIN 3 = a0 , O[1].1<0> ;
PIN 4 = b0 , O[1].1<1> ;
PIN 5 = c0 , O[1].1<2> ;
PIN 6 = d0 , O[1].1<3> ;
PIN 7 = a1 , O[1].2<0> ;
PIN 8 = b1 , O[1].2<1> ;
PIN 9 = c1 , O[1].2<2> ;
```

PIN 10= d1 , O[1].2<3> ;

shows how a single integrated circuit with two functional elements, consisting of an output port O[1] and a macro Read, may be represented. Assuming that these declarations are part of the description of a dual ROM, it is perfectly feasible for the two elements to share common pins, ports and macros. For example, they may both share a common address port A[1]. These extended names may be used in any of the contexts in which simple names are valid.

6.7.2 Global names

Any macro,port,bus or pin within a description may also be assigned a (secondary) name, termed a global name. This extended naming has been introduced to improve clarity within a description and for convenient programming in the hardware description language (HDL) and realisation software which uses the chip data base. Global names assigned within the chip description may be used in hardware descriptions without knowing that in a particular chip it corresponds to, say, I[1] and in another chip to I[2]. The realisation software assumes that global names are assigned in a consistent manner and that, for example, the name 'Par_in' used on a variety of chips will always be attached to similar ports (in this case the parallel input).

Global names which are to be assigned to a pin, port, bus or macro must precede the declaration to which they apply and themselves have a particular declaration syntax. Constructed from letters, digits and the underscore (_), providing that they start with a capital letter and are unique, a global name declaration must be preceded by a percent symbol '%' and followed by an assignment sign '=':

%Clock = PIN 1 = +ck ;

This declares a control pin ck which is activated by a positive edge. The pin may be referred to by its pin number (1), its pin name (ck) or by its global name (Clock).

The declarations:

        %Datain.1 = PORT I[1].1<1> = Read.1;
        %Datain.2 = PORT I[1].2<1> = Read.2;

declare two occurrences of the input port I[1]. Input port I[1] may be referred to as I[1] or Datain. The first occurrence of input port I[1] may be referred to as I[1].1 or Datain.1 and the second occurrence of input port I[1] may be referred to as I[1].2 or Datain.2. Similarly, the pin associated with the first occurrence of input port I[1] may be referred to as I[1].1<0> or Datain.1<0> and the pin associated with the second occurrence of input port I[1] may be referred to as I[1].2<0> or Datain.2<0>.

It must be stressed that if an object is to be given a global name on a multi-element chip then that name must be associated with each object on each element as shown in the example. If an attempt is made to confuse the design system by attaching element numbers to a global name and assigning them to different object types:

        %data.1 = PORT I[1]<4>;
        %data.1 = PIN 4 = junk;

or to assign global names to objects with different extensions

        %test.1 = PORT I[1].2<4>;
        %test.2 = PORT I[1].1<4>;

then the compiler will generate error messages. Therefore, as well as simplifying transfers in the HDL descriptions, the global name principle is used to relate similar functions and objects in an ICDL description with more than one element.

6.7.3   Clock signal declaration

The actions and conditional expressions which are associated with control pins, macros and ports state how the integrated circuit can be
used in a pseudo-synchronous application. However, if the integrated
circuit is to be used in a synchronous application, the shape of the
clock signals must be defined fully. Any control pin may be declared
as a synchronous clock pin simply by stating the clock signal level
during each time period which forms one cycle of the synchronous clock
waveform.

The simple declaration:

        PIN 1 = a ;

declares a control pin named a. The extended declaration:

        PIN 1 = a{H,L} ;

declares pin 1 to be a synchronous clock pin in addition to being a
conventional control pin. The list of signal levels (high or low levels), separated by commas ',' and surrounded by braces '{' and '}' defines the level of the synchronous clock signal during each time
period in one cycle of the synchronous clock waveform. The above example simply states that pin 1 must go 'up and down' during alternative
time periods.

The declaration:

        PIN 2 = b{H,L} : WIDTH = 20 ;

declares pin 2 to be a synchronous clock pin in addition to being a
conventional control pin. In addition, the minimum pulse width must be
greater than 20 ns. Therefore, each of the periods, specified in the
list of signal levels, must be at least 20 ns long.

However, there are integrated circuits which can only be operated in a synchronous manner and the clock waveform must be present at all times. These integrated circuits are described by extending the syntax of the pin declaration to include another special pin type called CLOCK. For example, the declaration:

        PIN 3 = c{H,L,L,L},CLOCK ;

declares pin 3 to be a synchronous clock pin which must always have the specified synchronous clock waveform applied and hence cannot be used as a conventional control pin. This notation can also be used to describe an integrated circuit with a polyphase clock. For example, the declarations:

        PIN 1 = a{H,L,L,L} , CLOCK ;
        PIN 2 = b{L,H,L,L} , CLOCK ;
        PIN 3 = c{L,L,H,L} , CLOCK ;
        PIN 4 = d{L,L,L,H} , CLOCK ;

declare a 4 phase synchronous clock system. The individual pin declarations illustrate how the 4 clock signals are arranged with respect to one another.

It is illegal to declare a set of clock pins with different repetition rates. Therefore, the two declarations:

        PIN 1 = a{H,L} , CLOCK ;
        PIN 2 = b{H,L,L,L} , CLOCK ;

must be re-expressed as:

        PIN 1 = a{H,L,H,L} , CLOCK ;
        PIN 2 = b{H,L,L,L} , CLOCK ;

6.7.4   Actions involving more than one time period

The port and macro actions, which have been declared so far, have only involved one time period. However, in the description of some of the more complex LSI circuits, it is necessary to specify a port or macro action which involves more than one basic time period. To overcome this problem, a port or macro action may be specified as a sequence of complex expressions separated by commas (,). The declaration:

        Load = b, +a&b ;

declares a macro which involves two time periods. If macro Load is enabled during period T, the following actions must be taken during the individual time periods:

        1) action b must occur during period T.
        2) action +a&b must occur during period T+1.

Therefore, when a port or macro is enabled, the first complex expression must occur during that period and any other complex expressions must occur during later consecutive time periods. However, this sequence of events can be changed by the inclusion of an asterisk (*) which denotes the action for time period T. The declaration:

        Write = c, *c&+d, c ;

declares a macro which involves 3 time periods. If macro Write is enabled during period T, the following actions must be taken:

        1) action c must occur during period T-1.
        2) action c&+d must occur during period T.
        3) action c must occur during period T+1.

The multiple action can replace any of the single actions previously described but it is illegal to declare a multiple action involving

166

more than one asterisk (*). However, if a macro action involves more than one time period, it cannot be used as a macro in another port or macro action. A single action may appear with or without an asterisk, e.g.

        Load = *+b
        and
        Load = +b

are identical.

If a conditional expression is applied to a port or macro declaration with a multiple action then the number of conditional expressions must equal the number of actions. It is illegal to include an asterisk in a conditional expression.

The declaration:

        PORT I[1]<1> = a, *a&+b-, a : VALID = 1, B, 1 ;

declares an input port with an action involving 3 time periods. If port I[1] is enabled during period T, then the following actions and conditions must apply:

        1) Period T-1: Action a always valid.
        2) Period T : Action a&+b- valid if B is enabled.
        3) Period T+2: Action a always valid.

6.8   COMMENTS

Within an ICDL description there is provision for two types of comments. The first is the usual IDES form of comment: preceded by a '/*' pair and terminated by a '*/' pair:

        /* This is the form of a discarded comment */

This type of comment is stripped out at the lexical analysis phase.

A second form of comment is provided to allow for text which it may be useful to access from the database query programs. This type of comment is denoted by the use of surrounding double quotes:

"This is the form of a stored comment"

and is stored by the compiler in the chip database.

Whilst ordinary comments may be written anywhere, stored comments may only appear in certain restricted places and contexts. These places are:

1) Preceding the chip description. A comment placed here is associated with the overall chip and would usually be used to describe the operation of the chip. (From the database query software this comment is extracted by entering the query 'comment chip').

2) Preceding the semi-colon in an object (port,pin etc) declaration. Comments entered in this manner apply to the object declared in that statement.

In general, comments may be of any length and take as many lines as are required for the description, provided that the syntactic rules of the description are not broken. The declaration:

I[1]<4> = Load "This is a 4-bit parallel input port" ;

is an example of an input port declaration with an associated comment.

All the comments which appear in the ICDL description may be individually extracted from the integrated circuit library using the database query software.

6.9   AUTOMATIC EXPANSION ALGORITHMS

The ICDL description may include a list of simple algorithms which describe how a port can be expanded by connecting two or more of the same type of circuits together. These algorithms can be used by design programs automatically to produce a circuit containing the number of chips which are required to realise any port width specified by the designer.

The expansion algorithm:

```
EXPAND =
{
        MODULO I[1], O[1];
        COMMON A[1], gr, gw, clock ;
};
```

associated with a 4-bit RAM, describes how it may be expanded to produce a RAM with the required bit width.

The EXPAND list is the list of rules which have to be obeyed in order to carry out the expansion and is surrounded by braces ({ and }).

The MODULO list is a list of objects which are expanded by the module of their width (I[1] and O[1] in this example). This means that if this particular chip was expanded to two chips then the resulting input and output ports would be twice as wide (i.e. 8 bits).

The COMMON list is the list of port names, data book pin names or assigned port or pin names which must be connected individually together when more than one integrated circuit is involved. In this example pin 'gr' is defined to be 'COMMON'; thus if pin 'gr' is pin 3 then pin 3 on every chip in the expansion would be connected together (VCC and GND are automatically assumed to be common).

If the above expansion algorithm is used to produce an 8-bit RAM, then the address lines A[1] and the control pins gr, gw and clock will have to be connected together individually to produce a circuit with an address port A[1], three control pins gr, gw and clock and a double width (i.e. 8-bit) input port I[1] and a double width output port O[1]. The blackbox will then contain two of the circuits described in the associated ICDL description. The remainder of the expansion algorithm is given over to describing the individual connections which are necessary in order to make the expansion function.

The CONNECT list is a list of port to port or pin to pin connections which must be made in the expansion. These connections state the method of connecting different pins on successive chips (or elements on chips) in order that the created circuit will function correctly.

Expansion algorithms define how two integrated circuits can be connected to produce a "super chip", i.e. a blackbox with the characteristics of an single integrated circuit but in reality it consists of two integrated circuits. This can be repeated (i.e another chip added by making the appropriate connections) to produce another "super chip" consisting of an individual integrated circuit and the previous "super chip", i.e. a blackbox which effectively contains three integrated circuits. Certain keywords are used to simplify the blackbox transfers in such a way as to remove any need for absolute numbers in the expansion. This allows the algorithm to be applied equally well to individual integrated circuits and to the resulting "super chips". The keywords provided represent the

    most significant circuit(MSC),
    least significant circuit(LSC),
    most significant element(MSE),
    least significant element(LSE),
    most significant bit(MSB),
    and
    least significant bit(LSB).

For example, a more complex expansion algorithm might be:

```
EXPAND = {
        MODULO I[1],O[1];
        COMMON clr,s0,s1,clk;

        LSC.O[1]<MSB>     ->      MSC.I[2]<0>;
        MSC.O[1]<LSB>     ->      LSC.I[3]<0>;
        .srsi             ->      LSC.srsi;
        .slsi             ->      MSC.slsi;
};
```

This algorithm, as well as specifying that I[1] and O[1] expand with the module of their width and that the pins clr,s0,s1 and clk are common to all chips in the expansion, also details 4 connections that must be made. The first specifies that the most significant bit on output port one on the least significant chip should be connected to (connections are directed) bit 0 on the second input port of the most significant chip. Similarly a second connection is to be made from the most significant chip to the least significant chip. These connections represent the chaining of bits in the expansion of a bidirectional shift register. The last two connections are present to declare signal assignments on an already expanded chip. i.e. having connected two chips together the 'srsi' (shift right serial input) pin on this 'super chip' is actually the 'srsi' on the least significant chip in the expansion.

6.10   THE REALISATION PROGRAM

Realise is the program which takes an HDL description of an algorithm and attempts to realise it using elements from libraries of predefined chips and designs. In one respect realise is a compiler for HDL descriptions, and checks their semantic and syntactic correctness. This is necessary because HDL files may have been generated manually, or may have been edited since being generated by the implement program. As may be expected, realise is written in C and uses a YACC generated parser utilising the common IDES lexical analyser.

The first action performed by realise is to create all the other IDES processes which it will need in its operation. Realise works by interrogating the chip and design databases using the quest and attribute programs, and performs boolean operations on logic expressions using logic, reduce, and follow. These programs are discussed in appendices II-IV. Thus the appropriate processes are created at the outset to ensure that realise will not be suspended for lack of the ability to create a process when it is actually required. These programs are used in exactly the same way as a human designer would use them, i.e. asking questions of them or giving requests to them in textual format, and receiving replies in textual format.

Having created the required processes, realise then parses the HDL file. The parser first of all includes any #include files, and parses the graph name and header to check for ports which are too big for the realisation software, have inconsistent bit widths, or are defined more than once, and it identifies any input and output bus ports. It then identifies each of the declared elements and sets up data structures for them. It interrogates the quest program to find the characteristics of any elements which are designs, and enters them into the data structure. This information comprises not only the internal characteristics of the element, but also its port and pin information.

Having successfully parsed the graph, and dealt with the elements realised as designs, the remaining elements must be designed from the chips available in the chip database. All undefined ports are given the default size, and then the process of selecting chips begins. This process consists of sending specifications to the attribute program taken from the HDL descriptions, and receiving replies which indicate which chips in the database are suitable, or failing that, any which can be expanded to be suitable. If multiple realisations are available, then the designer is asked to select one of them, or an automatic selection can be made. The data structure for the element is loaded with the relevant characteristics, and the port and pin information. If a realisation is using multiple chips, then the connections between common and interconnected pins are identified and entered into the structure. When all the chips have been selected and their details entered into the data structures, the transfer connections can be made. Simple full port transfers just require the appropriate port connections to be made in the data structure. Any undefined transfers can be made tri-state, open-collector, or multiplexor, and a suitable mode is selected and the details entered into the structure along with the enable information for the transfer. Multiple chip transfers are expanded across all the chips.

It is now possible to convert port tranfers to pin interconnections. At this point reduce is used to expand the actions on the pins into their basic signal form, removing macro actions and generating the optimum logical actions for the signals.

The control bistables are then entered into the data structure to complete this phase of the realisation. Currently the realisation of the control graph logic is rather primitive in that it assumes a directed-graph type of realisation. That is to say that it assumes that data operators are initiated by the control signals and also signify their terminations. This results in a realisation with bistables associated with each operator, initiating the operator and upon termination setting the following bistables which in turn control their operators. Further work needs to be done for synchronous control, including the incorporation of more detailed timing information into the system. Microprogramming realisations would need a complete new control realisation section to be written for the program.

The realisation program finally outputs the CDL file, a textual description of the realisation in the CDL language.

6.11   THE CIRCUIT DESCRIPTION LANGUAGE CDL

The header of a CDL file is the normal HDL header, but the data declarations list the chips and the designs selected for the realisation
of all the operators and cells. As can be seen in figure 6.18, chips
and designs are declared using the appropriate keywords chip or design
followed by the relevant identifier and the names of all entities
realised with this type of chip or design. For data operators or
cells which are realised with chips having multiple elements per chip,
the name of the chip is followed by the bracketed name of the cell or
operator with a letter appended to indicate which element is the one
being used, 'a' being the first, 'b' the second, and so on. Units
which are realised using multiple chips have a numeral appended to
their name to indicate this, 1 being the least significant and more
significant chips increasing in number. This is shown below:

```
chip     sn74193 aluout1, aluout2,
                 pcin1, pcin2, pcin3, pcin4;
chip     sn7474  stopped(stoppeda,);
```

The above describes the registers aluout, requiring two 74193 chips,
pcin, requiring four 74193 chips, and stopped, requiring one element
from a 7474 chip.

The data transfers form the next part of the description. Signals
from and to the control logic are preceded by a (') to differentiate
them from data transfers. For the control of data transfers the signals come directly from the control bistables and their identities are
listed in a later phase of the description, the activation signals.
The overall design is treated as a black box with a set of pins, and
the pins are numbered increasing from 1. The numbers are associated
with the design inputs and outputs in the order in which they are declared in the design name. These pins are indicated in the CDL
language by being preceded by a period (.). Thus

```
mul(multip<16>,multic<16>: result<32>)
```

has input pins .1 to .16 associated with multip, pins .17 to .32 associated with multic, and pins .33 to .64 with result. The transfers
indicate the logical conditions under which a conditional transfer is
made.

```
('loadres & out1.15) -> .33
```

indicates that the 'loadres signal from the control circuit, ANDED
with the data cell out, element 1, pin 15, goes to design output pin
33, and is a wired-or connection. The constructs :

```
-T>
-O>
-M>
```

indicate tri-state, open-collector, and   multiplexor   connections
respectively, whilst level control signals are indicated by:

```
->
-L>
-+>
-->
```

which indicate high true level (default), low true level, +ve edge or
-ve edge respectively.

```
H
L
GND
VCC
```

on the left-hand-side of transfers indicate that the pins are permanently connected to high or low levels, or Vcc power or ground

respectively. The realisations for the logic signals assume Nand,
Nor, and Inverter gates are available, and use the program 'logic' to
generate the expressions.

The next phase of the description gives the signals which connect
into the control logic (signals preceded by a '). These are the activation signals mentioned previously. Finally the control circuitry
is output. Each data operator has a similarly named control bistable
associated with it, having p (true) and q (false) outputs, and j and k
inputs, all bistables being clocked by the system clock. Connections
to the control bistables themselves are preceded by a $ symbol.

The blockhead and blockend bistables are BH and BE respectively, and
any bistable not directly associated with a named data operator (eg
syntax ands) is given a unique ordinal number starting from 1. The
control of the blockhead circuitry is output, guaranteeing that the
design is initiated correctly.

```
/* The multiplier after realisation */

mul(multip<16>,multic<16>:result<32>)
{
        /* Data Declarations */
        chip    sn7474  carry(carrya,);
        chip    sn74193 b1,b2,b3,b4,count1,count2;
        chip    sn74194 a1,a2,a3,a4,out1,out2,out3,
                out4,out5,out6,out7,out8;
        design  tstc    tstc;
        design  add     add;

        /* Data transfers */
        ('loadres&out1.15) -> .33;
        ('loadres&out1.14) -> .34;
        ('loadres&out1.13) -> .35;
        ('loadres&out1.12) -> .36;
        ('loadres&out2.15) -> .37;
        ('loadres&out2.14) -> .38;
        ('loadres&out2.13) -> .39;
        ('loadres&out2.12) -> .40;
        ('loadres&out3.15) -> .41;
        ('loadres&out3.14) -> .42;
        ('loadres&out3.13) -> .43;
        ('loadres&out3.12) -> .44;
        ('loadres&out4.15) -> .45;
        ('loadres&out4.14) -> .46;
        ('loadres&out4.13) -> .47;
        ('loadres&out4.12) -> .48;
        ('loadres&out5.15) -> .49;
        ('loadres&out5.14) -> .50;
        ('loadres&out5.13) -> .51;
        ('loadres&out5.12) -> .52;
        ('loadres&out6.15) -> .53;
        ('loadres&out6.14) -> .54;
```

```
('loadres&out6.13) -> .55;
('loadres&out6.12) -> .56;
('loadres&out7.15) -> .57;
('loadres&out7.14) -> .58;
('loadres&out7.13) -> .59;
('loadres&out7.12) -> .60;
('loadres&out8.15) -> .61;
('loadres&out8.14) -> .62;
('loadres&out8.13) -> .63;
('loadres&out8.12) -> .64;


H -> carry.1;
('tstc&tstc.17) -> carry.2;
!'tstc -+> carry.3;
H -> carry.4;
GND -> carry.7;
H -> carry.10;
H -> carry.11;
H -> carry.12;
H -> carry.13;
VCC -> carry.14;


('initb&.18) -> b1.1;
H -> b1.4;
H -> b1.5;
GND -> b1.8;
('initb&.20) -> b1.9;
('initb&.19) -> b1.10;
!'initb -L> b1.11;
H -> b1.12;
H -> b1.13;
L -> b1.14;
('initb&.17) -> b1.15;
VCC -> b1.16;
```

```
('initb&.22) -> b2.1;
b1.13 -+> b2.4;
b1.12 -+> b2.5;
GND -> b2.8;
('initb&.24) -> b2.9;
('initb&.23) -> b2.10;
b1.11 -L> b2.11;
H -> b2.12;
H -> b2.13;
b1.14 -> b2.14;
('initb&.21) -> b2.15;
VCC -> b2.16;

('initb&.26) -> b3.1;
b2.13 -+> b3.4;
b2.12 -+> b3.5;
GND -> b3.8;
('initb&.28) -> b3.9;
('initb&.27) -> b3.10;
b2.11 -L> b3.11;
H -> b3.12;
H -> b3.13;
b2.14 -> b3.14;
('initb&.25) -> b3.15;
VCC -> b3.16;

('initb&.30) -> b4.1;
b3.13 -+> b4.4;
b3.12 -+> b4.5;
GND -> b4.8;
('initb&.32) -> b4.9;
('initb&.31) -> b4.10;
b3.11 -L> b4.11;
H -> b4.12;
H -> b4.13;
```

```
b3.14 -> b4.14;
('initb&.29) -> b4.15;
VCC -> b4.16;


0 -> count1.1;
'deccnt -+> count1.4;
H -> count1.5;
GND -> count1.8;
0 -> count1.9;
0 -> count1.10;
!'initcount -L> count1.11;
H -> count1.12;
H -> count1.13;
L -> count1.14;
!0 -> count1.15;
VCC -> count1.16;


H -> count2.1;
!count1.13 -+> count2.4;
!count1.12 -+> count2.5;
GND -> count2.8;
H -> count2.9;
H -> count2.10;
!count1.11 -L> count2.11;
H -> count2.12;
H -> count2.13;
!count1.14 -> count2.14;
!'initcount -> count2.15;
VCC -> count2.16;


H -> a1.1;
H -> a1.2;
('inita&.1) -> a1.3;
('inita&.2) -> a1.4;
('inita&.3) -> a1.5;
```

```
('inita&.4) -> a1.6;
a2.15 -> a1.7;
GND -> a1.8;
(!'shifta|'inita) -> a1.9;
('shifta|'inita) -> a1.10;
H -> a1.11;
VCC -> a1.16;


a1.1 -L> a2.1;
a1.12 -> a2.2;
('inita&.5) -> a2.3;
('inita&.6) -> a2.4;
('inita&.7) -> a2.5;
('inita&.8) -> a2.6;
a3.15 -> a2.7;
GND -> a2.8;
a1.9 -> a2.9;
a1.10 -> a2.10;
a1.11 -> a2.11;
VCC -> a2.16;


a2.1 -L> a3.1;
a2.12 -> a3.2;
('inita&.9) -> a3.3;
('inita&.10) -> a3.4;
('inita&.11) -> a3.5;
('inita&.12) -> a3.6;
a4.15 -> a3.7;
GND -> a3.8;
a2.9 -> a3.9;
a2.10 -> a3.10;
a2.11 -> a3.11;
VCC -> a3.16;


a3.1 -L> a4.1;
```

```
a3.12 -> a4.2;
('inita&.13) -> a4.3;
('inita&.14) -> a4.4;
('inita&.15) -> a4.5;
('inita&.16) -> a4.6;
H -> a4.7;
GND -> a4.8;
a3.9 -> a4.9;
a3.10 -> a4.10;
a3.11 -> a4.11;
VCC -> a4.16;

!'initout -L> out1.1;
H -> out1.2;
('add&add.33) -> out1.3;
('add&add.34) -> out1.4;
('add&add.35) -> out1.5;
('add&add.36) -> out1.6;
out2.15 -> out1.7;
GND -> out1.8;
(!'shiftout|'add) -> out1.9;
('shiftout|'add) -> out1.10;
H -> out1.11;
VCC -> out1.16;

out1.1 -L> out2.1;
out1.12 -> out2.2;
('add&add.37) -> out2.3;
('add&add.38) -> out2.4;
('add&add.39) -> out2.5;
('add&add.40) -> out2.6;
out3.15 -> out2.7;
GND -> out2.8;
out1.9 -> out2.9;
out1.10 -> out2.10;
```

```
out1.11 -> out2.11;
VCC -> out2.16;

out2.1 -L> out3.1;
out2.12 -> out3.2;
('add&add.41) -> out3.3;
('add&add.42) -> out3.4;
('add&add.43) -> out3.5;
('add&add.44) -> out3.6;
out4.15 -> out3.7;
GND -> out3.8;
out2.9 -> out3.9;
out2.10 -> out3.10;
out2.11 -> out3.11;
VCC -> out3.16;

out3.1 -L> out4.1;
out3.12 -> out4.2;
('add&add.45) -> out4.3;
('add&add.46) -> out4.4;
('add&add.47) -> out4.5;
('add&add.48) -> out4.6;
out5.15 -> out4.7;
GND -> out4.8;
out3.9 -> out4.9;
out3.10 -> out4.10;
out3.11 -> out4.11;
VCC -> out4.16;

out4.1 -L> out5.1;
out4.12 -> out5.2;
('add&add.49) -> out5.3;
('add&add.50) -> out5.4;
('add&add.51) -> out5.5;
('add&add.52) -> out5.6;
```

```
out6.15 -> out5.7;
GND -> out5.8;
out4.9 -> out5.9;
out4.10 -> out5.10;
out4.11 -> out5.11;
VCC -> out5.16;

out5.1 -L> out6.1;
out5.12 -> out6.2;
('add&add.53) -> out6.3;
('add&add.54) -> out6.4;
('add&add.55) -> out6.5;
('add&add.56) -> out6.6;
out7.15 -> out6.7;
GND -> out6.8;
out5.9 -> out6.9;
out5.10 -> out6.10;
out5.11 -> out6.11;
VCC -> out6.16;

out6.1 -L> out7.1;
out6.12 -> out7.2;
('add&add.57) -> out7.3;
('add&add.58) -> out7.4;
('add&add.59) -> out7.5;
('add&add.60) -> out7.6;
out8.15 -> out7.7;
GND -> out7.8;
out6.9 -> out7.9;
out6.10 -> out7.10;
out6.11 -> out7.11;
VCC -> out7.16;

out7.1 -L> out8.1;
out7.12 -> out8.2;
```

```
('add&add.61) -> out8.3;
('add&add.62) -> out8.4;
('add&add.63) -> out8.5;
('add&add.64) -> out8.6;
H  -> out8.7;
GND -> out8.8;
out7.9 -> out8.9;
out7.10 -> out8.10;
out7.11 -> out8.11;
VCC -> out8.16;

a1.15 -> tstc.1;
a1.14 -> tstc.2;
a1.13 -> tstc.3;
a1.12 -> tstc.4;
a2.15 -> tstc.5;
a2.14 -> tstc.6;
a2.13 -> tstc.7;
a2.12 -> tstc.8;
a3.15 -> tstc.9;
a3.14 -> tstc.10;
a3.13 -> tstc.11;
a3.12 -> tstc.12;
a4.15 -> tstc.13;
a4.14 -> tstc.14;
a4.13 -> tstc.15;
a4.12 -> tstc.16;

b1.3 -> add.1;
b1.2 -> add.2;
b1.6 -> add.3;
b1.7 -> add.4;
b2.3 -> add.5;
b2.2 -> add.6;
b2.6 -> add.7;
```

```
b2.7 -> add.8;
b3.3 -> add.9;
b3.2 -> add.10;
b3.6 -> add.11;
b3.7 -> add.12;
b4.3 -> add.13;
b4.2 -> add.14;
b4.6 -> add.15;
b4.7 -> add.16;
out1.15 -> add.17;
out1.14 -> add.18;
out1.13 -> add.19;
out1.12 -> add.20;
out2.15 -> add.21;
out2.14 -> add.22;
out2.13 -> add.23;
out2.12 -> add.24;
out3.15 -> add.25;
out3.14 -> add.26;
out3.13 -> add.27;
out3.12 -> add.28;
out4.15 -> add.29;
out4.14 -> add.30;
out4.13 -> add.31;
out4.12 -> add.32;

/* Test signals */
carry.5 -> 'carry;
(((((count1.7|count2.3)|count1.6)|count1.3)|count1.2)
        -> 'le5;

/* Activation signals */
$add.p -> 'add;
$tstc.p -> 'tstc;
$inita.p -> 'inita;
```

186

```
$initb.p -> 'initb;
$loadres.p -> 'loadres;
$initcount.p -> 'initcount;
$initout.p -> 'initout;
$deccnt.p -> 'deccnt;
$shiftout.p -> 'shiftout;
$shifta.p -> 'shifta;

/* Control Circuitry */
$BE.q&.i&!'end0 -> $BH.j;
!.i ->$BH.k;
$BH.p&$BE.q&.i -> 'start0;

'start0 -> $initout.j;
initout.t -> $initout.k;

'start0 -> $initcount.j;
initcount.t -> $initcount.k;

'start0 -> $initb.j;
initb.t -> $initb.k;

'start0 -> $inita.j;
inita.t -> $inita.k;

$5.p&$6.p&$7.p&$8.p|'end1 -> '1;
'1&'count -> 'start1;

'start1 -> $deccnt.j;
deccnt.t -> $deccnt.k;

'start1 -> $shifta.j;
shifta.t -> $shifta.k;

'start1 -> $shiftout.j;
```

```
shiftout.t -> $shiftout.k;

$1.p&$4.p -> 'end1;

$shifta.p&shifta.t -> $tstc.j;
tstc.t -> $tstc.k;

$2.p&$3.p -> '2;
'2&'carry -> 'start2;
'2&!'carry -> 'start3;

'start2 -> $add.j;
add.t -> $add.k;

$add.p&add.t -> 'end2;

'start3 -> 'end3;

'1&!'count -> $loadres.j;
loadres.t -> $loadres.k;

$loadres.p&loadres.t -> 'end0;

'end0|$BH.p&!.i -> $BE.j;
$BH.p&!.i -> $BE.k;
$BH.p&$BE.p -> .t;
!$BH.p&$BE.p -> .f;

('end2|'end3) -> $1.j;
$1.p&$4.p -> $1.k;

$tstc.p&tstc.t -> $2.j;
$2.p&$3.p -> $2.k;

$shiftout.p&shiftout.t -> $3.j;
```

```
        $2.p&&$3.p -> $3.k;

        $decent.p&decent.t -> $4.j;
        $1.p&&$4.p -> $4.k;

        $inita.p&inita.t -> $5.j;
        $5.p&&$6.p&$7.p&&$8.p -> $5.k;

        $initb.p&initb.t -> $6.j;
        $5.p&&$6.p&$7.p&&$8.p -> $6.k;

        $initcount.p&initcount.t -> $7.j;
        $5.p&&$6.p&$7.p&&$8.p -> $7.k;

        $initout.p&initout.t -> $8.j;
        $5.p&&$6.p&$7.p&&$8.p -> $8.k;


}
```

FIG. 6.18.   Multiplier after realisation

CHAPTER 7
Conclusions

The basic IDES system as described has been implemented and is working for the design of computer systems, in particular those in which it is possible to introduce concurrency. Languages have been developed, and a variety of software tools have been implemented, which are used to interactively design, in a hierarchical manner, computer systems. A method of introducing suitable behavioural descriptions of digital circuits into a database has been developed, along with programs to retrieve and manipulate descriptions from this database. This enables designers or programs to perform circuit realisations at the hardware level.

Developments of IDES are taking place on several fronts. Although mainly concerned with integrated circuits, the chip database is equally applicable for use in the design of VLSI circuits themselves, using cell-based design systems. Unfortunately, cell libraries do not usually contain the type of information on cell behaviour needed by the database and its support programs. Cell libraries tend to contain information on the physical attributes of the cell, based on some graphical description such as EDIF [32]. However, cell libraries are now starting to be developed which contain behavioural models of their cells. It is at this level that IDES would choose to operate.

Another development has been in redefining and extending the top level language, G. This has been extended by including 'case' values with constants, comparisons, and numeric ranges. The model has been directed more towards modelling software, and the new language, SDL (System Design Language), has been implemented in PROLOG [33-34].

The concurrency aspects of the directed graph model are as applicable to software as they are to hardware. Considerable interest is now being shown in the problem of executing programs on parallel processor systems, even so-called massively parallel systems. One branch of IDES research is in applying analysis to software with a view to processing normal sequential programs into concurrent forms suitable for execution on such parallel systems. In some respects this may be regarded as a reversion to the original ideals of LOGOS of a CAD system for both hardware and software design. Since sequential software is usually written in a manner intended for execution on a von Neuman processor, it is often constructed so that it has to be executed sequentially. For instance, the index variable which is used in a loop and incremented at the end of the loop. Even though the index variable may be used only to specify which element of an array is being accessed on each pass through the loop, the fact that it is used and then modified before being used the next time round the loop means that the standard maximal parallelism software keeps these operations in sequence. It reads and uses the index value first and then writes it out incremented second. It therefore requires a higher level of intelligence to be applied to understanding what it is that the software is trying to do, and analyse it in the light of this knowledge. While the above simple problem has been tackled by optimising compilers for pipelined processors, the real benefit is to be obtained by applying concurrency over the whole program, including such localised situations. Hence PROLOG is being used in an effort to build a rule-based system for this application [35-36].

References

[1] Maxey G.F., Organick E.I. "CASL - A language for automating the implementation of computer architectures" Proc. 4th Int. Symposium on Computer Hardware Description Languages, Palo Alto, 1979, pp 102-108.

[2] "The ISPS computer description language" Dept. of Computer Science, Carnegie-Mellon University, PA 15213, CMU-CS-79-137.

[3] Zimmermann G., "VLSI design with the mimola design system" IEE European Conf. on Electronic Design Automation, 1981, pp 277-280.

[4] Rammig F.J. "The implementation of the computer hardware description language CAP and its applications" Proc. 4th Int. Symposium on Computer Hardware Description Languages, Palo Alto, 1979,pp 138-144.

[5] Anlauff H., Funk P., Meinen P. "PHPL - A new computer hardware description language for modular description of logic and timing" Proc. 4th Int. Symposium on Computer Hardware Description Languages, Palo Alto, 1979, pp 124-130.

[6] "Computer aided design language is a move toward universal hardware description" Electronics International, Jan. 13th, 1983, p92.

[7] Hill D.D. "ADLIB - A modular, strongly-typed computer design language" Proc. 4th Int. Symposium on Computer Hardware Description Languages, Palo Alto, 1979, pp 75-81.

[8] Schuler D.M. "A language for modelling the functional and timing characteristics of complex digital components for logic simula-

tion" Proc. 4th Int. Symposium on Computer Hardware Description Languages, Palo Alto, 1979, pp 54-59.

[9] "LDL logic design language" Dept of Computer Science, University of Manchester, U.K.

[10] "HILO" Cirrus Computers Ltd., High Street, Fareham, Hants, PO16 7AD, U.K.

[11] Silvar-Lisco, 3172, Porter Drive, Palo Alto, CA 94304, U.S.A.

[12] Peterson J.L. "Petri nets" Computing surveys, Vol. 9, No. 3, Sept. 1977, pp 223-252.

[13] Karp R.M., Miller R.E. "Parallel program schemata" Journal of Computer and System Science, pp 147-195, Vol.3, May 1969

[14] Slutz D.R. "Flowgraph schemata" ACM Conf. on concurrent systems and parallel computation, 1970, pp 129-141.

[15] Campos I., Estrin G. "SARA aided design of software for concurrent systems" AFIPS proc. N.C.C., Anaheim, 1978, pp 337-347.

[16] Glaser E.L. "Introduction and overview of the LOGOS Project" Case Western Reserve University, 1970

[17] Foulk P.W., McLean J.A., Mason R.A., O'Callaghan P.J. "AIDS - An integrated design system for digital hardware" IEE Proc. Vol. 127, Pt. E, No. 2, Mar. 1980, pp 45-54.

[18] Bain D. "A relationship between maximal parallelism and maximal simultaneity in a directed graph model of parallel computation" Electronic Letters, Vol 11, 1975.

[19] Coffman E.G, Denning P.J. "Operating system theory" Prentice-Hall, New Jersey, 1973.

[20] Dijkstra E.W. "The structure of the T.H.E. operating system" CACM Vol. 11 no. 5, May 1968 pp. 341-346.

[21] Heath F.G., Rose C.W. "The case for integrated hardware/software design, with CAD implications" Case Western Reserve University, 1971.

[22] Howard B.V. "Parallel program schemata and their hardware implementation" Digital Processes, pp 183-206, Vol.1 no.3, 1975.

[23] Manugian V. "Directed graph methods applied to the design of digital computers" Ph.d. Thesis, Heriot-Watt University, 1975.

[24] Ritchie D.M., Thompson K. "The UNIX time-sharing system." CACM, Vol.17, No.7, July 1974, pp.365-375.

[25] Kernighan B.W., Ritchie D.M. "The C programming language" Prentice-Hall Software Series, 1978.

[26] O'Callaghan P.J. "A language for the expression of parallel structure." Ph.D. Thesis, Heriot-Watt University, 1978.

[27] Bain D., Heath F.G. "A simplified method of establishing determinacy in a directed graph model of parallel computation" Electronic Letters, Vol.11, 1975.

[28] McLean J.A. "Computer aided design of digital systems" Ph.D. Thesis, Heriot-Watt University, 1978.

[29] Johnson S.C. "YACC - Yet another compiler-compiler" Bell Laboratories, Murray Hill, New Jersey.

[30] Warshall S. "A theorem on boolean matrices" JACM, pp 11-12, Vol.9 no.1, Jan.1962.

[31] Texas Instruments Ltd. "The TTL data book for design engineers" 1977.

[32] "EDIF Electronic design interchange format" EDIF steering committee, 1984.

[33] Heath F.G., Foulk P.W., Li D.Y. "Analysis and restructuring of concurrent systems using PROLOG" IEE Proc. Vol. 131, Pt. E, No. 5, Sept. 1984, pp 169-176.

[34] Heath F.G., Foulk P.W., Li D.Y. "System design language for the combination of data flow and control flow graphs" Software and microsystems, Vol. 2, No. 6, Dec. 1983, pp 142-146.

[35] Foulk P.W. "Directed graph models and their application to software development" Software and microsystems, Vol. 1, No. 7, Dec. 1982, pp 192-199.

[36] Foulk P.W., Nasser S.M. "Maximal parallelism in FORTRAN-like memory recursion problems" Computer performance, Vol. 5, No. 2, June 1984, pp108-115.

APPENDIX I

The Overall Guide to Using IDES

In order that the project could be completed in a shorter space of time, and as an aid to debugging, the programs have been written to permit stand alone use. Most of the software in the system communicates using a textual interface. This means that many programs have a front-end which parses textual input. This task is carried out using YACC generated parsers which in turn call upon a common IDES lexical analyser. At a lower level, software debugging has been made easier through the use of common routines. These routines are resident in three libraries:

liba: general utility routines
libg: architecture level data structure manipulation
libc: component database manipulation routines

are used by all the IDES programs internally. Routines were written to handle all common (or repetitive) operations: character string manipulation, dynamic memory allocation, formatted printing and so on. A bonus to be gained from this approach is that throughout the IDES suite the user interface to programs remains relatively constant, giving standard methods of interaction, standard output and error formats.

The execution of any individual program may be modified by the use of a set of run time switches, as is common in most UNIX programs.

These switches are the same for all IDES programs and have consistent
interpretations. The only distinction is whether or not a program
utilises a particular switch.

I.1   STANDARD FILE EXTENSIONS

Many IDES programs need a file of data as input. If the filename
given has no extension (a period '.' followed by a string of characters) then programs append a default file extension and look for the
appropriate file. Similarly, the programs, when creating output files
form their names using these same standard file extensions.

      '.g'   Directed graph description
      '.log' Directed graph data structure
      '.hdl' Hardware description language
      '.cdl' Circuit description language
      '.icdl' Integrated circuit description language
      '.cct' Circuit wiring list

This facility allows the designer to refer to a design at all levels
by the one name (the stem without an extension). The names of intermediate files may remain unknown to the designer.   These files are
generally in textual form representing the languages used at various
levels of abstraction in the design process. This is done so that
they may be modified at any time using the normal text editor.

I.2   INTERACTION

A number of programs within the suite have been written purely to be
interactive, they take a line or lines of input and generate a textual
output for each input data set. These programs may be used from the
terminal (e.g. bernie : used to simplify boolean expressions) but
more frequently are used by other programs, information being
transmitted between the programs using the UNIX pipe mechanism. Other
programs require only occasional interactive input (the response to a

query). This form of input is restricted to either a yes/no answer or
a numeric value. An invalid response will simply result in the question being asked again. When asked a direct question by an IDES program, the user may, if he wishes to examine external data in order to
decide upon an answer, request the execution of any UNIX program. To
do this he merely precedes his typed response with an exclamation mark
('!'-pling). In this mode the software will interpret the line of input as a normal system command and carry out its execution. This allows the user to (for example) list his current file space, print a
file or files, edit data files etc. Once execution is over, the IDES
software will ask the original question. There is no loss of context
and no program data is affected, unless the designer is knowledgeable
and self-destructive.

I.3   ERROR REPORTS

All error messages are generated using common error handling mechanisms (routines). This means that the errors always have a similar
output format:

            program-name:entity:line-number:error-message

Since it is often the case that a user-activated program will itself
activate a number of other programs, error messages are preceded by
the name of the program which caused the error. If that program is
operating upon a particular entity, a design or a file name, then the
name of this entity will also be printed. Similarly, if the file is a
text file (of a number of lines) then the number of the line currently
being processed is given. An attempt has been made to make the error
message itself consistent and meaningful. Names (i.e. of objects
within a design) which appear in an error message are surrounded in
single quotes. If a particular error is deemed fatal, the error message will be followed by the statement 'FATAL' and the program will
tidy up its filespace, kill any child processes and exit. Further, a
fatal situation may occur in a child process yet the parent, the pro-

gram which gave rise to the spawning of the child, may be able to continue. In such a situation the child process and all its children
will exit, whilst the parent process would continue in the hope that
it need not use that child again. If this is not the case the parent
would die on its first child access. This situation happens rarely,
generally during program (not design) development, but could be caused
by the absence of a required process or a non-existent design member.

I.4   DIAGNOSTICS

Diagnostic messages have been embedded in much of the code of the system, in particular in common routines so that they may be picked up by
all programs. By default, these messages are not printed and need to
be turned on by the use of a run-time switch. As well as being useful
in program development, they have been left in since they are, in general, informative messages saying exactly what a program is doing at a
particular time. As such they may serve to reassure the system user
that, in the longer running programs, work is actually in progress.

Further levels of diagnostic information may be accessed by turning
the program into verbose mode. In this mode both verbose diagnostics
and verbose output are generated. The level of verbosity is determined by a numeric value. At present some programs support up to five
levels of verbose diagnostics and anything above level two will significantly extend the runtime of most programs.

I.5   MEMORY ALLOCATION

Memory allocation within the system is dynamic. For any particular
object type or storage method there are no fixed limits. The designer
may equally well have a design with many components and few connections or conversely few components and many interconnections. The
only limit being the total amount of memory available for data
storage. An exception to this ruling is the default bit width associated with an object. For programming convenience this has been made

constant, at least for the duration of a program. If the default value assumed is not sufficient (or is too large) the designer may override using a run-time switch.

I.6   SIGNALS

IDES software obeys all the standard UNIX terminal conventions for line editing (del,ctrl w,ctrl u etc.), end of text (ctrl z) and so on. Certain control sequences are passed to programs in the form of signals (software interrupts). A 'ctrl c', the standard interrupt signal, will cause program termination. This signal is caught by IDES programs, and causes an elegant exit; temporary files are removed, child processes are properly killed and their cpu usage times accumulated, and finally, after having printed any diagnostic and timing information required, the program will exit.

Certain long running programs have an inbuilt facility which allows the 'toggling' of the run-time switches during execution. The action associated with the normal 'quit' (ctrl q) signal has been modified. On receipt of this signal the program executes a special routine which reads lines of input. These lines are expected to be of the same syntax as is used at run time start to set switches. It is thus possible to turn on or off a facility (e.g. diagnostics) part way through a run. Exit from this mode is signified by typing a 'ctrl z' in response to the prompt. Though this feature is present and operative and can be used wisely and usefully in certain situations, the designer who knows little about the internal operations of the software is advised to avoid it completely. The disastrous effects of changing certain switches (e.g. implementation mode from hardware to software or changing the default bit width) are obvious. This facility can also be used to interrupt program running in order to execute another utility. This is done in the same manner as was discussed under the heading of interaction.

I.7   SOFTWARE AVAILABLE

The IDES suite comprises many programs, all of which may be used
directly from a user terminal but only some of which directly form the
user interface to the IDES design system. That is to say, certain
programs are used within the system to support other programs and
hence are used only indirectly by the user. Within this section each
program, its required input, function, and generated output will be
described in isolation and only later will inter-relationships and execution sequence be given. The system itself is organised into a
number of levels concerned with the differing levels of detail required in the design process and utilises a number of languages (G,
HDL, ICDL). A knowledge of this structure and the languages used is
assumed in the following descriptions.

I.7.1   attribute

This program is used for database search and selection. The program
is completely interactive and, given as input a number of attributes
or features which the designer desires in a component, will search the
database and return the names of all suitable chips or designs. The
input query structure is very simple and will allow specification of
both positive and negative attributes (negative attributes being
features which the component must NOT have) and for numeric specifications of bit widths, elements per chip and so on. These specifications can be given in the form of a boolean equation and successively
edited to expand or contract the search domain. A full description of
the program is given in appendix III.

I.7.2   bernie,reduce,logic

These programs are concerned with the handling of varying forms of
boolean expression. The first (bernie), is used to handle simple
reductions of normal expressions giving as output a reduced sum of
products form of the input expression. Reduce, on the other hand, is

an extended form of bernie, which will handle timing and signal expressions. Logic, like reduce, is an extension of the bernie philosophy, which as well as reducing the input expression will suggest the best way to implement it in terms of the standard logic functions available. Bernie and reduce have no expression memory and immediately forget the previous equation. Logic on the other hand stores multiple expressions so that the effects of changing the list of available gates may be noted upon the implementation. Logic has an inbuilt facility for generating schematic diagrams of simple combinatorial circuits so that they may be more readily appraised. These programs and their use are described in detail in appendix II.

I.7.3 determ

Level one architecture descriptions may be checked for determinacy using this program. It takes as input a level one graph data structure and if the design is deemed determinate 'marks' it appropriately. All level one programs know about graph 'marking' and enforce a strict program execution sequence upon designers. If conflicts are found then the names of the control/data nodes giving rise to the indeterminacy are printed in a semantic error message which indicates the form of indeterminacy detected.

I.7.4 display

Operating upon a graph data structure, this program will generate a picture of the control and data flows involved. If the design has been specified using interactive graphics then the display will reflect the original input form, otherwise (for textually input designs) the layout program will have to have been run on the structure. Display, whilst it will allow the selection of either control or data flows (default is both), simply traces the data structure and displays objects at specified x-y coordinate positions. The descriptions of the objects themselves are not built into the program but are stored in files so that they may be changed easily using the graphics editor and so that all programs generating pictures will always use the same standard set. The display program output takes the form of a device independent coding which can be piped to a number of device dependent programs each of which deals with a separate device. Pictures may be generated on any available graphical device, the decision being taken only at execution time.

I.7.5   gc

This is the compiler for the architecture level description language G. This program takes as input a file containing G statements and if no errors are detected generates a graph data structure. The only form of error detection supported is syntactic, semantic errors being detected by a separate program. This is done to ensure that semantic errors are treated in the same way regardless of the mode of input (textual or graphical).

I.7.6   icdl

This program is a compiler for the integrated circuit description language ICDL. After having checked that a description is valid the program installs it into the chip data base and updates the files used by the database search program. Only correctly compiled and installed descriptions may be accessed using the search and query programs.

I.7.7   implement

Level 1 architecture descriptions are taken to level 2 hardware descriptions using this program. Taking as input a graph data structure and using both internal rules and interactive input this program generates an HDL language description of the design. Interaction is restricted to enquiries about, for example, the bit-widths of objects in the design, and as much information as possible is taken from previously implemented sub-designs. The language of form output of the program utilises only a specified sub-set of the HDL and where names are required to be generated (e.g. transfer names) then these are formed from the names of related objects in the design, rather than generating unintelligible numerics or mnemonics.

I.7.8   layout

Operating upon a graph data structure, this program will create x and y coordinate values for nodes in the graphs so that they may be displayed graphically. The algorithms used for node placement are oriented towards forming a layout which is aesthetically pleasing. This basically follows the normal rules of placement algorithms by minimising connection lengths and crossovers. The layout program has been designed to handle semantically incorrect graphs so that they also may be displayed and the erroneous portions viewed.

I.7.9   maxpar

An optional level 1 operation which, based upon the defined data flow in the design, will reorganise the control flow to make it maximally parallel. Parallelism in this context is defined as carrying out as many simultaneous operations as are possible with the specified data flow (architecture). The control flow generated is guaranteed to be determinate if the original design was determinate and the program will refuse to operate upon a design which has not been marked as determinate by program 'determ'.

I.7.10   mx

When graphical output is not available, this program can be used to print out the connectivity information of a graph data structure. The connectivity information is printed in the form of a connectivity ma-trix with the names and types of the nodes given in each case. A further matrix gives the transitive closure of the connectivity matrix and thus gives indication of the inter-node paths. A '1' at any point (x,y) in this matrix signifies that there is a path from node x to

node y in the design. These matrices are given for both the control
and data flow portions of the description.

I.7.11 quest(cquest,dquest)

Database queries are made using this utility. The program itself is a
camouflage for two separate programs concerned with integrated circuit
queries and design queries. Queries are made upon one component at a
time (presumably selected using the attribute program) and the same
query syntax is used regardless of whether the query object is a chip
or design. The range and power of the query language is presented in
appendix IV. It should be stated that because of the complexity of a
chip description the cquest program operates upon a pre-processed library of chips whilst the design query program dquest simply refers
directly to the text files describing those designs already realised
(CDL files).

I.7.12 realise

This program forms both a compiler for the HDL language and the
mechanism for realising a design in terms of physical components.
Designs given in HDL form are made in terms of generic components
(memory, adder etc). This program, as well as checking the syntactic
correctness and semantic acceptability of a design, uses the database
search and query software to select suitable components for the circuitry. Having done this, the transfers made between the original conceptual components are converted to connections and activating signals
between discrete gating and pins on packages. The output from the
program is again textual in the form of a circuit description language
(CDL).

I.7.13 tx

This program will generate a textual description of a graph data
structure in the form of the G language. It is useful when interac-

tive graphics were used to generate the original design or when the design has been modified through the use of a program such as maxpar.

I.7.14 valid

Semantic analysis of architectural descriptions is carried out by this program regardless of the mode of input of the design. Initially, this program checks for cycles in the control graph and outputs errors if any are detected. No further checking is done in this case since the developed algorithms depend upon the correct structuring of the algorithm. Assuming that there are no cycles, the program continues to carry out checks for the valid connection of nodes in both the control and data flow descriptions. A valid design will have its graph data structure marked so that other programs can check this before they start processing.

I.8   PROGRAM EXECUTION

Although many of the IDES programs can be executed individually, there is a 'normal' path through the system for those who want to follow the IDES ideology. Initially, an architectural description is given in G. This is compiled using the 'gc' utility to form a graph data structure and then checked out using the 'valid' program. Assuming no errors, the user then checks the determinacy of the program using 'determ'. Inevitably running these programs will show up some errors and the initial description will have to be changed using the normal system text editor and the sequence then re-run. Errors, especially in control flow, are often not apparent from the textual representation and, at any point in this level 1 iteration, the 'layout' and 'display' programs can be used to generate a picture of the design. Once the design has been proven to be determinate, the designer, if he wishes, may optionally call the 'maxpar' utility to convert the control sequencing to maximally parallel form. The conversions made by this program are performed directly upon the graph data structure and a visual presentation of the now re-formed description can be generated either by using 'tx' or the 'layout' and 'display' combination.

Once a design is deemed correct at the architecture level, the designer should wish to start filling in the details of his design. He starts by calling 'implement' on the graph data-structure to generate an HDL description. This takes the design to level 2 in the system, the implementation level. At this level functional testing could take place through the use of simulation, although this is not currently offered in the IDES suite.

Complete and correct simulation, if this is done, is the sign for the designer to proceed to level 3, the realisation level, using the program 'realise'. This program takes as input the HDL description of level 2 and from it, using database information, selects components to form the design. The output from this program is in the form of a circuit description language (CDL) which represents a design as a set of boolean equations and interconnections. At this stage all objects in the design have been selected and connections (boolean equations) are specified between the physical packages or circuits. The only components which have not been specified are the gates represented by the boolean operators in the equations. These operators state only the type of gate that should be used (and, nand, xor etc.) but do not specify which package(s) in which they will be found. This is done so that the circuit description language actually gives a textual representation of the schematic (logic) diagram of the design. This gives a generalised flow for using the system:

```
                G language file <---- text editor -------
                        ¦                               ¦
                /----- gc -------- syntactic errors --->¦
               /        ¦                               ¦
              /    / valid ------ semantic errors ---->¦
    display <- layout <-   ¦                            ¦
              \    \ determ ------ indeterminate ----->¦
               \        ¦                               ¦
                \--- maxpar                             ¦
                        ¦                               ¦
                    implement                           ¦
                        ¦                               ¦
                HDL language file <-- text editor ------¦
                        ¦      \                        ¦
                        ¦          simul -- incorrect ---->¦
                        ¦      /                        ¦
                    realise
                        ¦
                CDL language file
```

The separate utility 'icdl' has to be run upon any chip description which is to be installed in the library. This may be done at any time, but should only be done by the design system supervisor (i.e. the person on whose shoulders the load will fall if designs do not work because of incorrect chip descriptions). Other unmentioned utilities (bernie, reduce, logic, attribute, quest) can be run at any time, as and when they are required. They are guaranteed not to modify any database or design information and so can be used with complete immunity, even whilst the design software is active.

Programs developed for the design suite are stored in one common directory ("u1/ides/bin"). This is the case since many IDES programs 'spawn' each other and therefore must know where each other may be found. In many cases although the designer has only typed the name of

one program, he has brought into being a number of different programs.
To carry out a design realisation, for example, the designer executes
the program 'realise' with an argument specifying the design name.
Moments later there are ten executing processes:

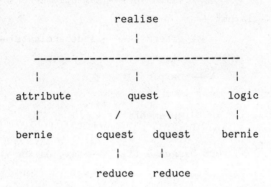

As can be seen certain of these (logical) processes are duplicated
(bernie,reduce) and are in fact multiply executed. IDES relies upon
the operating system to ensure that these are not in fact discrete but
simply different data spaces operated upon by a shared program text.
Child processes are executed immediately the parent is summoned. This
is done to ensure that they exist and will be present when required
thus avoiding a situation where a parent runs successfully for a long
time and then is forced to abort due to a lack of support. Most of
the children will remain in 'swap space' for the duration of the run
and by careful programming their excursions into main memory are kept
low. As many accesses as possible are made to a child in a contiguous
manner (i.e. without interspersing calls to other children). This is
also dependent upon the amount of memory available and the number of
other processes running. On a system with low memory and a large
number of active processes the IDES suite can be guaranteed to cause
furious swapping.

I.9   RUN-TIME SWITCHES

Run-time switches are provided to modify the action of a program at

the start of execution. The presence of a switch is signified by
preceding it with a plus ('+') or minus ('-') sign. These characters
distinguish a switch from a possible file name argument to the program. A file which is to be used with any IDES software must not have
a name beginning with either of these symbols. Preceding a switch
name with a plus sign is interpreted as turning on the switch whereas
the minus sign implies switching off. The switches themselves are,
without exception, single characters. Any further characters or digits are taken as arguments to the switch itself. Each switch must be
separated from its neighbour by a space and thus a space cannot be
used within a switch or file name. Every program in the system has
its own set of default switch positions (switches are by nature
binary, on or off, though there are varying degrees of being on).
These defaults are set prior to the interpretation of any settings
given by the user and so may be overridden. Although not all switches
are used by all programs, the setting or unsetting of an unused switch
is treated as a null operation and errors are only generated when a
totally unrecognisable switch is encountered. A simple example of
switch operation might be:

        layout +d -o +t filename

This example calls the layout program into execution turning on the
diagnostic(d) and timing(t) switches, turning off optimisation(o) and
operating on 'filename'. Switches and files are processed in strict
sequence, therefore in the previous example the diagnostic and timing
switches will both be on when the file is processed. This concept is
extendable to the processing of multiple files:

        layout +d file1 +t file2

Here the program is called with diagnostics turned on upon file1 and
then with both diagnostics and timing upon file2. Note that the
switch states remain the same through the processing of a file i.e.
switches are not reset to their default after processing a file. If

this was not desired then the command:

        layout +d file1 -d +t file2

would have to be used.

  Certain switches are mutually exclusive. For example, the switches
used to signify realisation mode (hardware, software, firmware). If
any one of these switches is turned on, then the others will automatically be turned off.

  The remainder of this section treats each switch individually and
gives some idea of its general function. Optional arguments to
switches will be shown in square brackets ('[',']'), though the brackets are not typed when using the arguments:

I.9.1 +/-d[fname]   diagnostic

The debug or diagnostic switch. When switched on this will cause the
printout of diagnostic messages giving the current state of the program. In general, these messages reveal the type of processing which
is taking place. Normally, these reports are made to the diagnostic
stream and they do not interfere with the normal output of the program. If the optional argument 'fname' is given, then a file of that
name will be created and the diagnostics sent there instead.

I.9.2 +/-f   force

This switch is used to force a program to continue past errors. Certain programs, in particular those that parse large quantities of
text, will exit upon having detected a number of errors in the parsing
phase. This switch can be used to override and continue. It should
only be used if you know the software intimately. The force switch
will not override a fatal error. The switch is used, for example, by
the layout program so that the designer may force the layout of a

graph which is known to be invalid.

I.9.3 +/-i   interaction

Certain programs may wish to ask the user for information. This
switch, the interaction switch, will tell the program whether or not
to allow interaction. If interaction is disabled (-i) then the program will make some decision as to a reasonable or acceptable answer.
The type of question governed by this switch is typified by the implementation program asking what form of transfers (tri-state, open-
collector etc.) a designer wishes to use on a bus. The switch itself
has   no   effect on those programs that are purely interactive
(bernie,reduce,quest etc) since this would effectively turn the programs into no-op's.

I.9.4 +/-1   listing

The listing flag is used by programs which parse textual input to give
a listing of the lines of input as they are being parsed. The line is
printed character by character, symbol by symbol as they are recognised by the lexical analyser. This mechanism allows the detailed
pinpointing of errors within a line of input (the normal error mechanism only gives the error and line number). Characters are printed as
they are read in. If subsequently they are pushed back on an internal
stack, they are wiped from the screen and are only restored when re-
used (the listing mechanism is not very efficient and will noticeably
effect the run time of a program).

I.9.5 +/-m   monitor

As has been discussed earlier, certain programs spawn other programs
in order that they may be used to process or supply information for
the master program. Communication between these processes is made in
a textual form in all cases. This switch, the monitor switch, will
cause the print out of all inter-process i/o between a parent and its

212

children.   This   information will always go to the same output stream
as diagnostic information. As with all   options   which   generate   extraneous output, this will noticeably affect run-time.

I.9.6   +/-o   optimisation

The optimisation switch. Every program which obeys this   switch   has
its own interpretation of what 'optimal' is, in the context of its own
processing task. Operation is best explained by example.   In   normal
mode, the graph layout program will carry out a layout based upon connection length. If the optimise switch is on, each line will be com-
pared with every other and cross-overs minimised. In many programs
optimisation is not fully used (understood), but it is a simple matter
to arrange/change a feature so that it is (not) carried out in optimisation mode and the repertoire will be extended through use.

I.9.7   +/-p   print

This flag is very definitely a software debugging flag and is recognised by those programs which have an internal data structure of some
note. When turned on, it will cause a print out of this   data   structure.   Intrinsic to this print out is the fact that the data is stored
in real addresses and these will be printed.   The   output   generated
when this flag is used is exceedingly long and has, in the case of a
simple design, been 100 pages.

I.9.8   +/-q   quiet

When turned on, this flag causes programs to go into quiet mode. This
means that errors, other than fatal errors, will not be reported.   In
general child processes are spawned in quiet mode.

I.9.9   +/-r   recurse

Implemented only in a limited form in a limited   number   of   programs, the recurse flag will cause programs to recurse down through the hierarchical levels in a design. The most successful use of this feature is seen in the display program, which, having displayed a particular design graph, will allow the user to select a node within that design and display it.

I.9.10 +/-t   timing

This flag being on will cause the timing of all processes. Every diagnostic message produced by the process will be preceded by the real time since the start of execution. As well as accumulating figures for real time, times are stored for the cpu usage attributable to the user process directly and its use of operating system facilities. At the end of execution a summary of pertinent (real, user, system) times is printed. Distinction is made between time attributable to the parent process and to its children, and totals are given for each.

I.9.11 +/-v[number]   verbose

This flag will cause the generation of verbose output. The output affected is both the normal textual output and the diagnostic output from a program. The optional number which may follow the switch command sets the level of verbosity (the default being one) and governs exactly how much information is printed. The highest level used to date is level 5 and at this level verbose diagnostics are printed out from the lexical analysers for every character read. Verbose diagnostics of lower numeric value are used to subdivide the status messages produced by the ordinary diagnostic switch. If verbosity is turned on without normal diagnostics being turned on then it will affect only the normal output of a program.

I.9.12 +/-y   yacc

This switch is used to turn on the specific diagnostics within the yacc parser portion of a program. These diagnostics give information

about the current state of the parser and which tokens are being processed at any time. Parser diagnostics are quite lengthy, a number
being generated for every symbol, punctuation mark etc. in the input
text.

I.9.13 +/-C,+/-D   control, data

These mutually exclusive flags are used to tell a program that it need
only consider the control or data portions of a description, the default being both. Certain programs must consider control in the light
of data-flow and vice-versa and so will ignore the flag.

I.9.14 +/-F,+/-H,+/-S hardware, firmware, software

Mutual exclusion is again used on these flags which select between the
firmware, hardware or software implementation and realisation of a
design. This project has been carried out with particular respect to
hardware design (the default), but 'hooks' have been left in the
software for future development of firmware/software generation.

APPENDIX II

Boolean Expression Manipulation

This appendix describes programs used within the IDES system to perform the manipulation of boolean expressions and extended expressions involving timing constraints. In principle each program takes an input line containing an expression and produces a modified output expression. The parsing of input is handled by a YACC generated parser and utilises the standard IDES lexical analyser to discriminate between tokens. Further, the tools all use standard IDES routines and thus are consistent in their production of diagnostics,verbose output, yacc parser diagnostics, run timing etc.

The programs are all written to be used from a terminal and will prompt for input (a colon ':' is used), however the programs check to see if they have been executed in another manner (e.g by another IDES program) and in this case will turn off prompting. Since certain of the programs produce more than one line of output for a given line of input, a null character is entered at the end of each output response. This does not affect the terminal usage of the program but is essential for maintaining synchronisation when programs are communicating. As well as input expressions, certain programs will accept commands which modify their action. These take the form of a single word written in place of an expression. The rule for evaluation of an input line is that if the first word on a line is a command word to the program, then that line is a command line. Otherwise it is an expression for evaluation. If the command word is preceded by a minus sign('-')

then this is interpreted as a request to turn off (or subtract) a particular feature.

Errors detected by the programs fall into a number of broad classes: syntactic,semantic,processing and fatal. The syntax of an error message is the same throughout IDES:

program_name:file_name:line_number:error_message

Any of the fields of the message may be omitted (for instance if input is not from a file then no file name can be given) and the message may be followed by the message 'FATAL' in which case the program exits. If it is desired, the reporting of non-fatal errors may be turned off by entering quiet mode at execution time (+q switch).

Consistency is again maintained in the symbols used to represent boolean operators. All programs accept the following logic symbols:

!	NEGATE
&	AND
¦	OR
#	NAND
~	NOR
^	XOR
=	EQUIV
(	OPAREN
)	CPAREN

A valid expression could therefore be

a&(b¦c)^!d

and this would be interpreted as:

a and (b or c) exclusive-ored with the negation of d

Similarly there is a set of symbols used to represent the basic signal types:

```
        HIGH (default is high)
!       LOW
+       POSITIVE EDGE
-       NEGATIVE EDGE
/       EXPANDABLE HIGH
\       EXPANDABLE LOW
```

and a valid variable could therefore be

\a+

which would represent a signal a which, having gone down before the time period (expandable low), must have a positive edge at the end of that same period.

Timing constraints may be represented in the following form:

{p/q:r/s}

where the variables p,q,r,s are integers representing respectively the leading edge setup, leading edge hold, lagging edge setup and lagging edge hold times. (N.B. the characters '{' ':' '}' thus have special meaning). Times may omitted for either the leading {:r/s} or lagging {p/q} edges or for both. If it is necessary to represent multiple timing constraints e.g. for both ordinary(O) and low power schottky(LS) options on a chip this may be done:

{O,L = p1/q1:r1/s1,p2/q2:r2/s2}

where the first set of timing constraints (p1/q1:r1/s1) apply to the first option (O). Again any particular edge may have no constraints.

Any symbols that do not have special significance to a program may be used to create the name of a variable. This means, for example, that if a program does not manipulate timing constraints then (by virtue of the expression syntax) timing symbols will be assumed to be part of the variable name and manipulated accordingly.

The most complex variable will be a symbol name with specified leading and lagging edge signal types and with multiple timing constraints.

e.g. −a+{O,S = 2/3:4/5,1/2:1/2}

and any number of these may be bound together by the use of boolean operators to form an expression.

II.1   bernie

Bernie (Boolean Expression Reduction, Negation and Implicant Expansion) is used to produce a sum of prime implicants from the given input expression. No attempt is made to remove non-essential prime implicants and therefore the resulting expression is not necessarily in minimal form. A sample bernie session might be:

```
%bernie
:!(!a¦!b)¦!b&(b¦a)
a
:a^b^c
!c&b&!a¦!c&!b&a¦c&!a&!b¦c&b&a
:
```

II.2   reduce

Reduce is an expanded form of bernie and is used to produce a sum of
products of expressions involving signal types and timing. As such
the program is much larger than bernie and can handle only the AND,OR
and NEGATE operators. One further difference in operation is the interpretation of the NEGATE operator(!). An occurrence of NEGATE can
be treated either as meaning complement (default) or invert and interpretation mode can be changed at will by typing the commands 'invert' or 'complement'. The difference in interpretation can be seen
in the example script:

```
%reduce
:!/a\
!a
:invert
:!/a\
\a/
:
```

Reduce will produce a sum of products for every complex expression
given:

```
%reduce
:a & (b{1/2:3/4} | c{5/6})
a&b{1/2:3/4} | a&c{5/6}
:
```

If that timing which pertains to a particular option alone is required, it may be obtained by using the selection operator '*':

```
:a & (b{1/2:3/4} | c{0,L = 5/6,7/8}) * L
a&b{1/2:3/4} | a&c{7/8}
:
```

220

It should be noted that in this example the lagging edge setup and
hold times for 'c' have been omitted - as may be done anywhere - and
that the timing constraints specified for 'b' have not been tied to
any particular option and are thus assumed to hold true for all.

II.3   follow

Follow is used to test the compatibility of two consecutive signals
and to generate the net signal for the present time period. To do
this, follow expects not a boolean equation but simply a comma
separated pair of signals representing the two signals present at time
T-1 and T (the current period) respectively:

```
%follow
:a+,+a
+a
:/a\,/a\
a\
:\a/,\a/
a/
:
```

The output for each of the examples given is the net signal. Although
there are no signal types directly corresponding to a\ and a/, they
behave in a similar manner to /a\ and \a/ when used as the past signal
in the calculation of the net present signal. If any of the input
signals had been of incompatible types, a '0' would have been generated and if their timing constraints were incompatible then a '1' would
be the result.

An extension to follow allows additional information to be given in
order to define the width of the time period in which the specified
signals are active. The command:

```
a{0/3} , -a
```

generates the signal '-a' because it assumes that the width of the past time period (i.e. the time period when the signal a{0/3} is enabled) and the width of the present time period (i.e. the time period when -a is enabled) are infinite. However, if the past time period width is less than 3 time units then the signal sequence given should generate a '1'. The duration of past and present periods may be added in the following manner:

```
%follow
:a{0/3} , -a : 3 , 3
-a
:a{0/3} , -a : 2 , 3
1
:
```

Since the width of the past and present time periods is normally the same, the command:

```
a{0/3} , -a : 3 , 3
```

may be abbreviated to

```
a{0/3} , -a : 3
```

II.4   logic

Logic is a program aimed at the realisation of boolean expressions with logic gates. It does this in terms of the logic gates that it is told to use, and the maximum number of inputs permitted on a gate. It may be given this information at any time by issuing commands:

```
%logic
:nand 2
:nor 3
:invert
:
```

This tells the logic program that it may use 2-input nand gates, 3-input nor gates and inverters. Since there are many commands to the logic program, an abbreviated syntax allows complete specifications in one line:

```
%logic
:nand 2,nor 3,invert
:
```

If you wish to use only 2-input and gates, 2-input or gates and inverters, the command 'mixed' is a useful shorthand. Further, if there are no inverters, the program may be told to use another gate instead:

```
%logic
:invert nand
:
```

At any time the 'list' command can be invoked to list the types of gates which can be used. Unlike the other programs mentioned, 'logic' stores an input expression and thus if the environment is changed by the issue of a command(s), then it will reprocess the current expression within the new constraints.

The expression output format relies heavily on parentheses in order to determine the number of inputs on a specific instance of a gate type. Reverse polish notation output can be obtained. The command 'polish' will force the program to print expressions in this form with each operator being followed by the number of operands to which it applies (the default for inverter is one and for gates is two):

```
%logic
:(a&b&c)¦(d&!e)
((a#b#c)#(d#!e))
: polish
abc#3de!##
:
```

As can be seen from this example (in either output form) 'logic' sug-
gests one 3-input nand for a,b,c one 2(default)-input nand for d,!e
and so on.

By default, expressions are realised in the exact form in which they
are input. If however the 'optim' command is issued the expression
will be given a sum of products expansion and then a Quine-McLusky optimisation before realisation takes place:

```
%logic
:mixed
:(a&b&!c)¦(a¦!c)
(((a&b)&!c)¦(a¦!c))
:optim
(!c¦a)
:
```

Certain extra features have been added under pressure from users,
and, although they are never used by other programs in the IDES system, they may be found useful in stand-alone use. The first addition
was the ability to define sub-expressions. This is done using a pseu-
do assignment syntax:

224

```
%logic
:mixed
:a&b&!c
((a&b)&!c)
:*b = !(a¦c)
((a&b)&!c)
:interp
((a&!(a¦c))&!c)
:optim
0
:
```

In this example 'b' is defined (*b =) as being '!(a¦c)'. This, however, did not affect the output until the program was told to
interpret/interpolate sub-expressions ('interp' command). When this
command is issued, a parenthesised form of sub expression is interpo-
lated into the main expression. Operators within a sub expression may
themselves have attached definitions and as long as this never becomes
recursive (an operator defined in terms of itself) the nesting may be
infinite. As is shown in the last example, sub-expression interpola-
tions can change the complete nature of an expression. In this example optimisation shows that the expression now resolves to zero.

A second extension was provided for users who doubted the
reduction/realisation capabilities of the program and wanted some way
of proving that the output expression did indeed provide the same logic function as the input expression. This facility has been given in
the form of a truth table. A truth table may be called for at any
time by issuing the command 'truth'. The evaluation takes place on
the output form of the expression (i.e. after all manipulations) and
can handle all operators. An extension of this option allows the user
to obtain a modified truth table with a particular variable held at
zero or one. To hold a at zero during evaluation the 'truth' command
is followed by an optional comma separated list of settings in the
form 'a=0'. Truth value settings are held over from one evaluation to

the next and it is permitted to reset the value to a don't-care (both
zero and one) situation - 'a=*'.

```
%logic
:mixed,xor
:(a^b)&!c
((a^b)&!c)
:truth
    a   b   c
    0   0   0  - 0
    0   0   1  - 0
    0   1   0  - 1
    0   1   1  - 0
    1   0   0  - 1
    1   0   1  - 0
    1   1   0  - 0
    1   1   1  - 0
((a^b)&!c)
:truth c=0
    a   b   c
    0   0   0  - 0
    0   1   0  - 1
    1   0   0  - 1
    1   1   0  - 0
((a^b)&!c)
:optim,truth
    a   b   c
    0   0   0  - 0
    0   1   0  - 1
    1   0   0  - 1
    1   1   0  - 0
((((!c&b)&!a)|(((!c&!b)&a))
:
```

From this example, in its last two parts, it can be seen that the program does indeed produce logical equivalents of its input expressions.

APPENDIX III

attribute

This appendix describes a fast search facility provided under the IDES system for the selection of integrated circuits. Searches are made based upon a set of desired attributes specified by the user and the user is provided with facilities to modify (restrict or widen) his search pattern in order to home in on a suitable chip. In order to attain a reasonable speed, the program is designed to use only features which a chip 'may' or 'may not' have and does not allow for selection based on more variable features such as speed or power consumption.

III.1 THE SEARCH MECHANISM

Attribute takes as its working data a file which is produced and maintained by the chip library installation program 'icdl'. This file contains, for every chip in the library, a record of a finite maximum length (a compile time constant) which, as well as identifying the chip by name, holds information as to the nominal bit width of the chip, number of words, number of elements on a chip and number of pins on the package. Also recorded within this structure are the features which were specified in the 'TYPE' declaration in the chip description. The presence of a feature (attribute) is signified by the appropriate bit in a buffer of bits being set, and the interpretation that the program has of a particular position in the buffer is to be found in another file. This second file is termed the buzzword file

and the individual buzzwords are stored in buffer index order.   These
buzzwords are the keys which the user may specify as attributes when
carrying out his search.

III.2   THE SEARCH PROPER

The program itself obeys all the IDES conventions in terms of
switches, error message format, terminal i/o prompting, boolean operator conventions and so on.   A search is specified in terms of a set or
sets of desired attributes which in essence is a sum of products form
of boolean expression.

```
%attribute
:register&counter&bit=4
sn74169
sn74193
:
```

In this example a search has been carried out for a four bit counter
and (in a limited database) two chips which would fill the bill have
been suggested.   Within the expression the numeric relation bit=4 has
been used.   This type of relation may be used in a valid context only,
i.e. when referring to bits, words or elements in a package.   The
full set of numeric relations is:

```
<       less than
<=      less than or equal to
=       equal to
>=      greater than or equal to
>       greater than
```

If the user wanted to find out more about these chips, then he could
issue the command 'verbose'.   In response to this, the program would
print all the known attributes of the chips selected.

```
%attribute
:register&counter&bit=4
sn74169
sn74193
:verbose
sn74169
        ttl
        LS
        S
        enable
        synchronous
        load
        register
        counter
        up
        down
        bit=4
sn74193
        ttl
        O
        L
        LS
        synchronous
        load
        expandable
        register
        clear
        counter
        binary
        inc
        dec
        bit=4
    :
```

If it was desired to narrow down the search without doing this form of manual comparison of the chip features, then it is a simple matter to add further terms to the search expression.

```
%attribute
:register&counter&bit=4
sn74169
sn74193
:&enable
sn74169
:
```

In this example the search has been narrowed down by the 'anding' of the attribute 'enable'. By doing this, the user has said that the 4-bit counter for which he is searching must have an enable function provided. Similarly, a search may be extended by adding further terms which would be acceptable alternatives.

```
%attribute
:register&bit=8
:|register&bit>=4&expandable
sn74193
sn74194
:list
        register&bit=8
        |expandable&register&bit>=4
:
```

In this example an unsuccessful search was initially made for an 8-bit register. On this failing, the user extended his search requirement by saying that an acceptable alternative would be a register of greater than 4 bits which had a specified expansion algorithm. Also shown is an example of the 'list' command which allows the user to have a look at the search expressions which he has to date specified.

Having specified search expressions, the user may amend the last expression to meet his requirements. This is done by adding or removing terms as is shown in this continuation of the last example:

```
        :&counter
        sn74193
        :list
                register&bit=8
                |expandable&register&counter&bit>=4
        :-counter
        sn74193
        sn74194
        :-bit
        sn74193
        sn74194
        sn7474
        :list
                register&bit=8
                |expandable&register
        :
```

In this example references to 'bit' and 'counter' have been removed by preceding the words with a minus ('-') sign. This creates a different situation to preceding a buzzword with a negate ('!') symbol since specifying '!counter' would tell the program that selected chips <u>must</u> <u>not</u> be counters whereas '-counter' simply removes any reference in the search to the attribute 'counter'.

It should be noted that such additions and deletions are always on the last expression given, but that the expressions may be moved around to make any one the last using the 'edit' command. This command takes an argument which specifies the number of the expression which you wish to edit (number order is the sequence in which expressions are shown as output to the 'list' command):

```
        :edit 1
        :list
                expandable&register
               |register&bit=8
        :-bit&bistable
        sn74193
        sn74194
        sn7474
        sn7475
        sn7477
        :
```

An expression may be deleted using the 'remove' command with an appropriate numeric argument. If all expressions are to be removed the 'wipe' command will do this.

Discussion so far has dealt with expressions as though the user were specifying each term(s) individually and successively. They can, however, all be specified in one complex expression provided that the program knows that this is desired. To do this the expression must be preceded by a slash '/'. On recognition of this syntax the program will do an internal wipe (remove all previous expressions) and also carry out a sum of products expansion on the input:

```
        %attribute
        :/register&(counter|decoder)&bit>=4&(clear|preset)
        sn74193
        :list
                register&clear&counter&bit>=4
               |register&preset&counter&bit>=4
               |register&clear&decoder&bit>=4
               |register&preset&decoder&bit>=4

        :
```

As usual, these expressions may be individually edited or removed at will.

A number of other commands exist which give information about the program and how to use it. The command 'chips' will list all chips currently available in the database, the command 'buzzwords' will list all the words in the buzzword file, the command 'keywords' will tell of all the words which have special significance to the program.

If a particular chip name appears too frequently in your searches and it is known that the chip is not desired, then the 'inhibit' command can be used to remove it from the list of available chips. Inhibited chips are restored to the active list whenever the 'wipe' command is issued (either explicitly or implicitly through the use of a '/' at the beginning of an expression).

APPENDIX IV

quest — Database Query

This appendix describes the query mechanism provided under IDES for chip or design database queries. Although chip and design information is stored in different forms and in different places, the query program provides a completely uniform interface to both types of description. To do this, queries are restricted to those which are applicable to the object (chip or design) as a whole, to the individual ports on the object or to the individual pins on the object. If a particular query has no valid interpretation for an object then it is not signalled as an error but simply generates no output text. Error messages are generated if reference is made to non-existent items or if a query is syntactically incorrect.

IV.1   THE QUERY MECHANISM

The program 'quest' is actually a dummy program which 'sits on top' (parent) of two discrete programs (children) which individually deal with chip and design queries and thus, without having one very large program, the different forms of storage of chip descriptions and designs may be reconciled. All the commands which will be described can be applied to both chips and designs. To save distinguishing between these throughout the text the generic term 'circuit' package will be used. Both the child processes (cquest and dquest) are written using Yacc and so are fairly large but, since only one is actually in use at any time, then size is not particularly crucial.

In order that quest may decide as to which program to send input
queries it is necessary that the user precede his initial query with
the type of package in which he is interested:

```
%quest
:design encode
:


or


%quest
:chip sn74193
:
```

Queries typed after this point will be passed directly to the appropriate program and answered. If, at any point, it is desired to
change the query package, then a similar command will activate the appropriate program and package loading. To find the name of the packages that have been selected, simply type the keywords 'design' or
'chip'. An after-affect of such a query is that the context is
changed to be that of the last query:

```
%quest
:design encode
:chip sn74193
:design
encode
:
```

In this example the user first asked to query on a design called 'en-
code' and then, without asking anything, set up for queries on the
chip 'sn74193'. The query 'design' which followed allowed him to find
which design he was querying and also means that queries which follow
will be directed to the design query program. The chip query program
however is already activated and loaded with the chip 'sn74193'. Ac-

cess to it may be made at any time by simply typing 'chip' to inform
the program of such an intent.

IV.2   QUERY FORMS

Legal queries have two basic syntactic forms. The first form is syntactically fixed and takes no arguments other than keywords. These
commands are termed special. The second command form allows for commands which take an argument(s) specifying the subject and object of a
query. As such, these commands are the most common and are termed
simply queries. For convenience and clarity, certain keywords are allowed a plural form (pin or pins). These plurals may be used anywhere
that the original keyword may be used and internally are mapped to the
singular form.

IV.2.1 Specials

Special commands have a fixed structure and are generally those
queries which pertain to the package as a whole. For example, typing
'speed' will give rise to the printout of the nominal operational
speed of a package (in the various available technologies). A
representative selection of these commands is:

attributes	—list all the attributes of a package
attributes symbol	—has a package a particular attribute(symbol)
option	—what technologies is package available in
option symbol	—is package available in particular technology
source	—print source description of package
speed	—nominal operation speeds of package
speed symbol	—nominal speed of particular technology
comment chip	—print any comments assoc. with package
no bit	—how many bits wide is package
no bus	—how many bus ports has package
no clock	etc.
no element	

```
no global
no macro
no option
no pin
no port
no power
no word
```

The 'special' queries are so simple to insert into the program that they are constantly being extended and it would be pointless to try and give a comprehensive list here. They are particularly useful to automated design programs which need to know how many pins(say) there are before asking for specific information on them.

IV.2.2 Queries

As has been mentioned earlier, queries take a specific form:

        question subject object

where each of the fields may contain a particular set of (key)words. In the following discussion each field will be treated separately and only then brought together as a whole. The full significance of a keyword may not be obvious, particularly with respect to chip features, and the reader is recommended to read the language descriptions of 'HDL' and 'ICDL', the respective language description chapters for designs and chips.

A question specification tells the program as to the type of information desired, and it may use any of the following keywords:

action	load
bit	macro
bname	modulo
bus	name
change	nochange
clock	number
comment	output
common	override
connect	pin
delay	port
drive	type
expand	valid
global	wait
initial	width
level	

A subject specification tells the program as to the form of the object specification which follows. This intermediate step to object specification is necessary only if there could be ambiguity as to which form of object was being investigated (e.g. a port and a pin with the same name) or if the answer form desired is different from the object form specified (e.g. the answer desired refers to a port whereas object specification is in terms of a pin). Valid subjects are:

    bus
    clock
    global
    macro
    pin
    port
    power

If 'subject' is omitted the program will make a guess rather than flag

an error. Should the guess be wrong, it is a simple matter to re-
enter the query in a more rigid form. This program can be used by
other programs to do database queries and in such an environment it is
recommended that explicit subject identification is given.

An object specification tells the program exactly which object the
query is about and may take one of a number of forms. These forms
depend on the allowable object types in the description languages and
there are many ways of specifying a particular object. If, for example, information about pin 12 on a particular package was desired, the
number '12' would be a valid object. If this pin had a known name, d1
say, then the text 'd1' would be a valid object also. Similarly, if
pin d1 were known to be bit 3 of input port 2 then the specification
'I[2]<3>' would be acceptable. The description languages allow secondary names to be assigned to objects such as ports,pins and macros.
These names are known as globals and the quest program allows them to
be used anywhere that their associated objects would have been valid.
If the port (I[2]) of the previous example had the global name
'par_in' then 'par_in<3>' would have identified the desired pin. A
more rigorous description of the object specification modes would be:

        global-
                GLOBAL_NAME
        port-
                global   (must be associated with a port)
                PORT_TYPE[PORT_NUMBER]
        pin-
                global   (must be associated with a pin)
                port<BIT_NUMBER>
                PIN_NUMBER
                PIN_NAME

Since a package may have a number of elements (e.g dual D_type bistable) the language descriptions allow for tagging a port name with
the element number which is of interest. Anywhere that a port may be

specified, it can be followed by an element number (the default is
one). In the context of the previous example, if the input port on
the second element of a package was to be specified, this would require the following:

par_in.2<3>

If object specification is omitted completely, then the program assumes that everything which satisfies the subject specification is of
interest. For example, the text 'name pin 12' will generate the name
of pin 12, whereas the text 'name pin' will generate a list of the
names of all the pins on the package. In all such cases of multiple
output, the lines are identified by another feature of the object (for
pins it would be their number).

IV.3   A SAMPLE QUERY SESSION

This section gives an example of a short query session using an
sn74193 as the query package. Those lines starting with a colon ':',
the query program prompt character, are typed by the user. All successive lines until another prompt are the responses of the program.

```
%quest
:chip sn74193
:attributes
ttl
register
counter
binary
synchronous
bit=4
```

242

```
:speed
O       25
L       3
LS      25
:name globals
Preset
Reset
Par_in
Par_out
Carry
Borrow
:type global Par_in
port
:type Par_in
I
:name Par_in
I[1]
:bit port Par_in
4
:pin Par_in
1
9
10
15
:action Par_in
\ld/
:valid Par_in
\ld/&count_down{O,L,LS=20/0,100/0,20/0}&+count_up
:expand Par_in
modulo
:expand port
I[1]    modulo
O[1]    modulo
```

```
:expand pin
4       connect
5       connect
11      common
12      connect
13      connect
14      common
:name pin 4
count_down
:connect pin count_down
.count_down     -> LSC.count_down
```

The session starts with the selection of the desired package ('chip sn74193') and the first real query is for a list of 'attributes'. The next query is an example of a special query where the user asks for the 'speed' of the package and is told that it is available in 3 forms (ordinary,low power and low power schottky) and given the appropriate speeds. Next a query has been made to 'name globals' and after having been given a list of these the user has homed in on a particular one and asked its 'type' and 'name' and found that it represents input port 1 (I[1]). Following this, the user has asked how many bits are in the port ('bit port Par_in') and what pins these are on the package ('pin Par_in'). Having found out this information, the next questions pertain directly to the in-circuit operation of the port. How to enable the port ('action Par_in') receives the response to ensure that the pin 'ld' is low at the time (\ld/). When will the port be 'valid' (when is it in a state to accept input) gets a complex signal expression involving three other objects (pins) on the package.

The remaining queries pertain to expansion of the package i.e. how, from an n-bit object, to form an m-bit object(m>n). Package expansion is defined within the package description by an expansion algorithm which basically consists of a list of those objects which should undergo a 'modulo' expansion (data lines), a 'common' connection (con-

244

trol pins and address lines) and those objects which require special
and dedicated 'connect' features (certain control pins). In the case
of this example, the query 'expand Par_in' has been made and the user
is told to carry out a modulo expansion on this port. At this point
queries are made about how to expand all ports ('expand port') and
pins ('expand pin'). The output from these queries gives examples of
all three expansion forms and after finding that the name of pin 4
('name pin 4') is 'count_down' the user has asked exactly how it
should be connected in the context of an expansion ('connect pin
count_down'). The resultant output indicates that pin count_down on
the current expansion element should be connected to the count_down
pin on the element of lesser significance (LSC - Lesser Significant
Chip).

This example shows only a limited number of features of the quest
program but it is hoped that it is enough to give the flavour of the
program.

APPENDIX V

The Formal Syntax of G

```
graph :=
        <header> <body>
header :=
        name [<params>]
params:=
        '(' [<namelist] ':' [<namelist] ')'
body :=
        '{' [<dc_dec>]* [<data_dec>]* <cg_part> '}'
dc_dec :=
        dcell <dc_list> ';' |
        dbus <db_list> ';'
dc_list :=
        <dcell> [',' <dcell>]*
db_list :=
        <dbus> [',' <dbus>]*
dcell :=
        name ['<'number'>'] ['=' number]
dbus :=
        name ['<'number'>']
data_dec :=
        type name <op_list> ';' |
        self <op_list> ';'
```

```
op_list :=
        <operator> [',' <operator>]*
operator :=
        name <params>
namelist :=
        name [',' name]*
cg_part :=
        [<arcset>]+
arcset :=
        <leftlist> ':' <rchain> ';'
leftlist :=
        ['<'] |
        [<leftlist> ',']* <node>
rchain :=
        <rightlist> [':' <rightlist>]*
rightlist :=
        ['>'] |
        [<rightlist> ',']* <node>
node :=
        <instance> |
        while [not] <test> [do <subgraph>] |
        if [not] <test> then <subgraph> [else <subgraph>] |
        switch <test> '{' [<case>]* '}'
test :=
        name ['.'number]
case :=
        case <namelist> ':' <subgraph> ';' |
        default ':' <subgraph> ';'
subgraph :=
        <node> |
        '{' <cg_part> '}'
instance :=
        name ['.' number] |
        '&' ['.' number]
```

V.1   AN EXAMPLE OF G

```
/*
Evaluation of the factorial function - iteratively

Algol equivalent:-
        x:=1; i:= n;
        WHILE i>0 DO
                BEGIN
                x := x*i;
                i := i-1;
                END
        ans := x;
*/



fact(n:ans)
{
        dcell    x=1,i;

        type transfer   lans(x:ans),li(n:i);
        self            dec(:i),mul(x,i:x);

        <:li:
        while i do {
                <:mul:dec:>;
        }:
        lans:>;
}
```

APPENDIX VI

The Formal Syntax of HDL

```
circuit:=
        <header> <body>
header:=
        name [<params>]
params:=
        '(' [<arglist>] ':' [<arglist>] ')'
arglist:=
        <arg> [',' <arg>]*
arg:=
        name [<bitwidth>]
bitwidth:=
        '<' number '>'
body:=
        '{' <declarations> <transfers> <control> '}'
declarations:=
        [<declaration>]+
declaration:=
        name [<attributes>] <instances> ';'
        self <instances> ';'
        NODECLAR ';'
attributes:=
        '(' <attriblst> ')'
```

```
attriblst:
        <attrib> [',' <attrib>]*
attrib:
        name
instances:
        <instance> [',' <instance>]*
instance:=
        name [<words>] [<bits>] [<initial>]
words:=
        '[' number ']'
        '[' '?' ']'
bits:=
        '<' number '>'
        '<' '?' '>'
initial:=
        '=' number
transfers:=
        [<transfer>]+
transfer:=
        <perm_tran> | <name_tran> | <test_tran>
perm_tran:=
        <tran> ';'
tran:=
        <xtran> [<time>]
xtran:=
        <connect> | <load> | <assert>
time:=
        '(' number ')'
connect:=
        <locn> [<bitspec>] '-' [<tranmode>] '>' <locn> [<bitspec>]
load:=
        <binlist> '-' [<tranmode>] '>' <locn> [<bitspec>]
assert:=
        name '.' name
```

```
tranmode:=
        T | M | O | ?
locn:=
        [<boxname>] ['.' <portname>]
boxname:=
        name
portname:=
        name | <portid> '[' number ']'
portid:=
        I | O | B | A | F
bitspec:=
        '<' <bitlist> '>'
bitlist:=
        <bitrange> [',' <bitrange>]*
bitrange:=
        <bitpos> ['-' <bitpos>]
bitpos:=
        MSB | LSB | number
binlist:=
        <binary> [',' <binary>]*
binary:=
        0 | 1
name_tran:=
        <tran_name> <tranlst> ';'
tran_name:=
        name '=' '='
tranlst:=
        <tran> [',' <tran>]*
test_tran:=
        <test_name> <exp> ';'
test_name:=
        name '=' <test_form> '='
test_form:=
        b | w
```

```
exp:=
        '(' <exp> ')'   |
        <exp> '&' <exp> |
        <exp> '|' <exp> |
        <exp> '^' <exp> |
        <exp> '=' <exp> |
        '!' <exp>       |
        <locn> <bitspec>


control:=
        [<arcset>]+
arcset :=
        <leftlist> ':' <rchain> ';'
leftlist :=
        ['<'] |
        [<leftlist> ',']* <node>
rchain :=
        <rightlist> [':' <rightlist>]*
rightlist :=
        ['>'] |
        [<rightlist> ',']* <node>
node :=
        <simple> |
        while <test_bit> [do <subgraph>] |
        if <test_bit> then <subgraph> [else <subgraph>] |
        switch <test_word> '{' [<case>]* [<defcase>] '}'
test_bit:=
        '(' <not> <andtype> ')'
test_word:=
        '(' <andtype> ')'
not:=
        not | '!'
case :=
        case <valist> ':' <subgraph> ';' |
```

```
valist:=
        <valno> [',' <valno>]*
valno:=
        number
defcase:=
        default ':' <subgraph> ';'
subgraph :=
        <node> |
        '{' <control> '}'
simple :=
        <andtype> | <synand>
andtype:=
        name ['.' number]
synand:=
        '&' ['.' number]
```

254

VI.1   AN EXAMPLE OF HDL

This HDL description is of a very simple 16 bit multiplier using the
standard shift-and-add technique to produce a 32 bit result. The
design itself has been interactively generated from an algorithmic
description previously specified in the language 'G'. The defaults
allowed in the language are heavily used, bit and port specifications
only being given where absolutely necessary.

```
/* This description has been implemented from G  */
/* and has a maximally parallel control graph.   */




mul(multip<16>,multic<16>:result<32>) {
        register(shiftl)      a<16>;
        register              b<16>;
        register(dec)         count<5>;
        register(clear,shiftl) out<32>;
        adder                 add<32>;

        /* Data Graph */
        b<0-15> -> add.I[1];
        out -> add.I[2];

        loadres == out -> .result;
        initb == .multic -> b;
        inita == .multip -> a;
        initcount == 16 -> count;

        add == add -> out;

        shifta == a.shiftl;
        shiftout == out.shiftl;
        deccnt == count.dec;
```

```
initout == out.clear;

count =b= count<0>|count<1>|count<2>|count<3>|count<4>;
carry =b= a<MSB>;

/* Control Graph */
<: initout,initcount,initb,inita;
initout: while(count) do {
        <: deccnt,shifta,shiftout;
        deccnt: >;
        shifta: tstc;
        tstc: if(carry) then ;
        carry: >;
        shiftout: carry;
};
count: loadres;
loadres: >;
initcount: count;
initb: count;
inita: count;
}
```

APPENDIX VII

The Formal Syntax of ICDL

```
chip:=
        <header> <body>
header:=
        [<comment>] name [<params>] [<options>]
params:=
        '(' [<namelist>] ':' [<namelist>] ')'
namelist:=
        name [',' name]*
options:=
        '[' [<optionlist>] ']'
optionlist:=
        <option> [',' <option>]*
option:=
        O ¦ L ¦ LS ¦ H ¦ S
body:=
        '{' <attributes> <defaults> <declarations> <expansion> '}'
attributes:=
        TYPE <attriblist> ';'
attriblist:=
        <attrib> [',' <attrib>]*
attrib:=
        name ['=' number]
```

```
defaults:=
        [<default> ';']+
default:=
        <speed> | <load> | <drive> | <width> | <output>
declarations:=
        [<macro>]* [<port>]* [<bus>]* [<pin>]*
global:=
        '%' <gnam> '='
gnam:=
        name <elemnum>
macro:=
        [<global>] <mnam> '=' <macrospec> [':' <func>]* [<comment>] ';'
mnam:=
        name [<elemnum>]
macrospec:=
        <mexp>
port:=
        [<global>] PORT <prnam> '=' <portspec> [':' <func>]* [<comment>] ';'
prnam:=
        <portid> '[' number ']' [<elemnum>]
portid:=
        'I' | 'O' | 'A' | 'F'
portspec:=
        <mexp> | <flist>
flist:=
        '{' [<macro>]* '}'
bus:=
        [<global>] BUS <bnam> '=' <busspec> [<comment>] ';'
bnam:=
        'B' '[' number ']' [<elemnum>]
busspec:=
        <prnam> '/' <prnam>
pin:=
        [<global>] PIN <pnum> '=' <pspec> [':' <func>]* [<comment>] ';'
```

```
pnum:=
        number
pspec:=
        [<sense>] <pnam> [<clocks>] ',' <cadnam>
sense:=
        '!' | '+' | '-' | '*'
pnam:=
        name
clocks:=
        '{' <clocklist> '}'
clocklist:=
        <clock> [',' <clock>]*
clock:=
        H | L
cadnam:=
        <prnam> <bitnum> |
        <specpin>
specpin:=
        VCC | GND | CLOCK
comment:=
        text
mexp:=
        <cexp> [',' <cexp>]*
cexp:=
        ['*'] <exp>
exp:=
        '(' <exp> ')' [<time>] |
        <exp> '&' <exp> |
        <exp> '|' <exp> |
        '!' <exp>
        <expobj> [<time>]
expobj:=
        <mnam> | <prnam> | <bnam> | <signam>
signam:=
        [<edge>] <pnam> [<edge>]
```

```
edge:=
        '+' | '-' | '/' | '\'
time:=
        '{' [<optionlist> '='] <timelist> '}'
timelist:=
        <times> [',' <times>]*
times:=
        [<intpair>] [':' <intpair>]
pairlist:=
        <intpair> [',' <intpair>]*
intpair:=
        <int> '/' <int>
intlist:=
        <int> [',' <int>]*
int:=
        number | '-' number
func:=
        <valid> | <change> | <nochange> | <override> | <delay> | <wait>
        <initial> | <speed> | <load> | <drive> | <output> | <width>
valid:=
        VALID '=' <mexp> | VALID '=' '?' | VALID '=' '?' '?'
change:=
        CHANGE '=' <mexp>
nochange:=
        NOCHANGE '=' <mexp>
override:=
        OVERRIDE '=' <mexp> | OVERRIDE '=' '?' | OVERRIDE '=' '?' '?'
delay:=
        DELAY '=' <mexp>
wait:=
        WAIT '=' <mexp> | WAIT '=' '?' | WAIT '=' '?' '?'
initial:=
        INITIAL '=' <initform>
initform:=
        H | L | X
```

```
speed:=
        SPEED [<optionlist> '='] <intlist>
load:=
        LOAD [<optionlist> '='] <pairlist>
drive:=
        DRIVE [<optionlist> '='] <pairlist>
output:=
        OUTPUT  '=' <outform>
outform:=
        TTL ¦ TRI ¦ OC
width:=
        WIDTH [<optionlist> '='] <intlist>
chipnum:=
        [<chipno>] '.'
chipno:=
        LSE ¦ MSE ¦ LSC ¦ MSC ¦ number
elemnum:=
        '.' <elemno>
elemno:=
        LSE ¦ MSE ¦ number
bitnum:=
        '<' <bitspec> '>'
bitspec:=
        LSB ¦ MSB ¦ number
expansion:=
        EXPAND '=' '{' [<expands>] [<connects>] '}' ';'
expands:=
        <elist>
elist:=
        [<edata>]*
edata:=
        <etype> <eobjs> ';'
etype:=
        MODULO ¦ COMMON
```

```
eobjs:=
        <eobj> [',' <eobj>]*
eobj:=
        <prnam> | <pnam>
connects:=
        <connlist>
connlist:=
        [<conndata>]*
conndata:=
        <cobj> '-' '>' <cobj> ';'
cobj:=
        <chipnum> <prnam> <bitnum> |
        <chipnum> <pnam>
```

VII.1   A SIMPLE EXAMPLE

This example gives a listing of the ICDL description for the SN74193 synchronous, 4-bit, up/down, binary counter. The description includes the circuit options O, L and LS, but for simplicity, the DELAY expressions have been excluded from the output port declarations.

```
sn74193[O,L,LS]
{
        TYPE  ttl,register,counter,binary,synchronous,bit=4;
        LOAD  O, L, LS = -1600/40, -180/10, -400/20;
        DRIVE O, L, LS = 1600/-40, 360/-20, 800/-40;
        SPEED O, L, LS = 25, 3, 25;
        WIDTH O, L, LS = 20, 200, 20;

        Inc     = +count_up & count_down{O, L, LS = 20/0, 100/0, 20/0}
                : OVERRIDE = Load | Clear;
        Dec     = +count_down & count_up{O, L, LS = 20/0, 100/0, 20/0}
                : OVERRIDE = Load | Clear;
%Preset=Load = \ld/
                : VALID = I[1]{O, L, LS = :20/0, :100/0, :20/0}
                : OVERRIDE = Clear;
%Reset= Clear = /clr\;

%Par_in=PORT I[1]<4> = Load
                : VALID = ?
                : OVERRIDE = ?;
%Par_out=PORT O[1]<4> = 1;
```

```
          PIN  1 = b,              I[1]<1>;
          PIN  2 = qb,             O[1]<1>;
          PIN  3 = qa,             O[1]<0>;
          PIN  4 = +count_down   : INITIAL = H;
          PIN  5 = +count_up     : INITIAL = H;
          PIN  6 = qc,             O[1]<2>;
          PIN  7 = qd,             O[1]<3>;
          PIN  8 = gnd,            GND;
          PIN  9 = d,              I[1]<3>;
          PIN 10 = c,              I[1]<2>;
          PIN 11 = !ld           : INITIAL = H;
%Carry= PIN 12 = !carry;
%Borrow=PIN 13 = !borrow;
          PIN 14 = clr           : INITIAL = L;
          PIN 15 = a,              I[1]<0>;
          PIN 16 = vcc,            VCC;


          EXPAND = {
                  MODULO I[1],O[1];
                  COMMON ld, clr;


                  LSC.carry        ->        MSC.count_up;
                  LSC.borrow       ->        MSC.count_down;
                  MSC.carry        ->        .carry;
                  MSC.borrow       ->        .borrow;
                  .count_up        ->        LSC.count_up;
                  .count_down      ->        LSC.count_down;
          };
}
```

N.B. Expandable pulse signals are used to declare macros Load and Clear, because they ensure that pins load and clear are only asserted while their corresponding macros are enabled.

Index